CONTENTS

PREFACE

P ublication of this study has been undertaken with several purposes in mind. Foremost among them is a desire that Iowa readers take a new look at their agricultural past and become concerned for the rich but dwindling number of buildings that reveal this heritage. In so doing, the book will, we trust, help prompt readers to report additional historical details about the barns mentioned here or to tell us about others we have missed — those that either still exist or once existed in Iowa. An immediate purpose of this study was to complete a thematic survey inventory of round and polygonal barns that may be eligible for listing on the National Register of Historic Places.

The book has its origins in farm-building bibliographic research carried out during the years 1976 and 1977 by the Division of Historic Preservation. This had, by mid-1978, expanded into a larger undertaking entitled "The Changing Iowa Farm: Agricultural History Through Buildings," a project combining large-scale bibliographic investigations, mail surveys, and research in farm building publications. Still in progress, the long-term project includes the publication of brief histories of farm building types in Iowa accompanied by a catalog of known examples. *Without Right Angles* represents the first in this projected series.

A study of Iowa's round barns offered a good beginning survey with which to test our ideas for the entire series all the way from initial research through final publication. Round barns as a type combined the virtues of being manageably small in number and having high intrinsic visual and historical interest.

In the early summer of 1978 we began, in an organized fashion, to identify round barns throughout Iowa. Since scant published information existed on the number and location of these barns, apart from the several noted in Wilson L. Wells, *Barns In the U.S.A.* (1976), we began by sending out mail questionnaires and searching for local informants. Leads came in from county agricultural extension agents, vocational agricultural instructors, county historical society members, owners of what the Iowa Department of Agriculture had designated as "Century Farms," and from listeners of Lee Kline, a farm broadcaster with WHO Radio in Des Moines. In time, the most important single contributor of leads proved to be

Cupola and loft of the Nebergall barn in Scott County are revealed in this 1979 photograph by Frank Hunter.

Karlene Kingery of Creston, Iowa, who has gathered information on many barns in the state as part of her project "The Iowa Barn — A Vanishing Landmark." Her sources of information helped to confirm site locations, to add details about the barns she had visited and to point toward other then-unconfirmed barns reported to her. As each round or polygonal barn came to our attention, we began a file on it and sent a mail questionnaire to the reported owner. Most of the owners kindly answered our inquiries and, in many cases, gave us valuable information. A later phase involved field work: taking photographs of each barn and confirming its location on a map. Frank Hunter, a professional photographer, carried out a major share of the field work, and his photographs comprise most of the visual material presented in this study.

The job of collecting information ultimately proved to be quite lengthy; at least it was far longer than we first anticipated. First of all, more barns turned up than the forty or so we had originally expected to find in Iowa. Our expectations had been based on the findings of Roger Welsch for Nebraska, in which he had located thirty-six round barns. This miscalculation turned the project from one that we had hoped, in the beginning, would be simply a matter of compiling information on forty barns into a labor of prolonged and intensive research on more than one hundred sixty. Second, we learned that conducting a statewide survey on a rural vernacular building consumes more time and expense than other kinds of surveys. For one thing, farm buildings — being of little concern to architects, historians, and art historians — have been ignored in the existing literature. This prolonged the time needed to place the buildings in a broader historical context, because the clues lay buried in brief references to advances in farm building design and construction in contemporary farm magazines, newspapers, and agricultural experiment station reports. Also, unless the building was highly conspicuous or unusual, local interest in the structure rarely reached beyond the family of its original owner to attract the attention of a rural newspaper editor, agricultural journalist, or writer of a town or county history. That gave us few knowledgeable informants to whom we might turn to learn where the many smaller and more isolated round barns might be in Iowa. So, instead of undertaking a job of matching up a rich literature with easily compiled instances of round barn construction in Iowa, we faced a long research task of ferreting out the locations of barns and interpreting them in a reasonable historical context. Additionally, the expense of travel to sites scattered about the state became, all too frequently, compounded by our returning home only to learn, within a short time, that another round barn stood close by one we had already visited.

In the course of time, many facts about the barns proved simply beyond the reach of our research. The investigative approach we pursued necessarily took us only so far. Financial costs of lengthy field work, for example, precluded much being done at the farm itself beyond fixing the location of each barn on a map and spending several minutes photographing the barn before going on to the next reported site. In so doing, we lost whatever additional meaning we might have gained from sketching the interior framing of the barn, especially the configuration of bents used in barns of heavy timber construction. Beyond field work, however, all too often our mail questionnaire and other sources offered little or no information about the round barn's past. Few of the barns have remained in the same family, and turnover in farm ownership and the rural population generally has almost guaranteed the gradual erasure of historical memory about the building.

Notwithstanding the difficulty and delay, we take considerable pleasure in having done the survey. Rural buildings, expecially old farm buildings, are fast disappearing from the scene, so we greatly appreciated the opportunity to study one type in an historical fashion. It is a wonder that, despite the decades-long absence of regard for farm architecture, we found so many formerly useful rural structures still standing across Iowa. Many buildings, albeit suffering from neglect and disrepair, undoubtedly owe their longevity to the fact that their owners have put off the hard work of reducing the stubborn structure to pieces for hauling away. Others stand in better shape because their owners find in them a link to, and a sense of continuity with, the work and accomplishments of their forebears. It is our hope that, by calling attention to how these shapes and types of farm buildings have come to be on Iowa farms, others will seek, when feasible, to preserve the state's most endangered species among them.

To a large degree, all works based on extended research are collaborative works in that they rest on both collective scholarship and the assistance of many others at all levels of preparation. As the historian in charge of the farm buildings research project, I have been responsible for the overall preparation of this report, but many people have contributed both research assistance and editorial suggestions that are reflected in the final draft of this volume. Although it is impossible, for example, to enumerate the many persons and groups upon whom I have relied for information about individual round barns, I am most grateful for the cordial help that farm owners extended to us.

Among the people directly employed on the survey, I want especially to thank Tamara Tieman for her contributions. Tieman brought to this undertaking a calm approach and sound judgement, as well as a warm interest in farm buildings history. From the beginning of her employment in late 1977, she had worked in various capacities as research assistant, editor, or writer on aspects of our farm buildings project. In mid- 1978, with the results of our several mail surveys indicating that numerous round barns existed in Iowa, Tieman ably assisted in carrying out some fall and early winter field recording on several round barns in Iowa. She later rejoined this effort fulltime during the summer and fall of 1979. While she spent much of her time during these months inventorying site information and coordinating the work of our contract photographer, she also undertook a broader task. Based on our research observations at that time, Tamara put together a twenty-three page draft report that reduced many of our oral discussions to writing and acted as a point of departure for later revisions. Several passages and ideas appear here nearly as they were expressed in this draft by Tieman. I would also like to acknowledge the work of our professional photographer, Frank Hunter. In addition to producing the numerous fine photographs that are found throughout this book, he collected many useful historical details about numerous barns and faithfully met every deadline we imposed upon him.

After the departure of Tieman and Hunter at the close of 1979, the project entered a phase of further background research in contemporary sources on round barn originators, popularizers, and builders. Simultaneously, phone calls and field work continued on matters related to newly reported round barn sites, and writing proceeded on what would eventually become a 105-page narrative. In this effort, several people kindly provided me with valuable information from unpublished materials and primary sources: Linda J. Harsin and Shirley L. Koch from Kansas on barn builder Benton Steele, Annette Frost and E. Kowal from New York on octagon barn popularizer Elliott W. Stewart, Ronald Chasse on the barn of Lorenzo Coffin, and H. Wayne Price on the Gordon-Van Tine Company. For his diligent research assistance and kind help in preparing the map of sites, I wish to thank Matt Hussman. Over the span during which this book was written, I also owe acknowledgement to Sarah J. Enticknap, and Cynthia Korshun who labored faithfully to enter the manuscript into the office word processor and make many subsequent revisions from successive drafts.

Finally, I wish to express my obligation and thanks to several colleagues in the Iowa State Historical Department and within the historical profession who gave generously of their time to read a draft of the study and offer general criticisms and detailed corrections and suggestions: Christie Dailey, William Silag, Tamara (Tieman) Robertson, Martha H. Bowers, Adrian D. Anderson, Jack Lufkin, and Ralph J. Christian. Alan Schroder deserves particular acknowledgement for his experienced copy-editing of the manuscript. His discerning eye caught many inconsistencies and grammatical errors that demanded correction and I greatly appreciated his several suggested improvements on my choice of words. The author, nevertheless, bears full responsibility for everything he has written.

Ryan Barn, Downey, Iowa   *M. Hayek '70*

Chapter One:

TIME AND PLACE

Secrest barn, just west of Downey, shown in a 1981 pencil drawing by artist Marjorie B. Hayek.

The round barn," cheered B. J. Diers in 1914, "is getting to be quite the thing out here in Iowa."[1] Its future seemed bright, indeed. After all, this carpenter and builder from Granville had just erected an immense ninety-foot version on a farm in northeastern Plymouth County and found, to his delight, "favorable comments" coming "from everyone who has seen it." And now, during the winter months, he was busy putting the finishing touches on a design for an eighty-four-foot model to be built in the spring.[2] Others shared his enthusiasm. A seventy-foot Iowa round barn with self-supporting roof, portrayed in the *Breeder's Gazette*, drew the editor's praise as being "solid as a rock" and "just the thing for a windy country."[3] Meanwhile, when the farm journal *Field Illustrated* featured a hollow-clay-tile version from Iowa, its editor acclaimed that "hundreds of Iowa farmers have taken a liking to barns of this design."[4]

Yet within a decade editorial and other support for the barns had evaporated, and today the traveler sees few of them across the state. Despite their relatively small number, however, one would be mistaken to dismiss the round barn as some fleeting expression of Americans' past eccentricity. Its story, in fact, illustrates far more — namely, the experimental phase of a movement that aimed to make farm practices more efficient and economical.[5]

What we think of as the "traditional" Iowa farm has in fact always known constant change. Today, for instance, the farmstead is increasingly horizontal, as farmers embrace long, sleek, metal, single-story pole buildings for housing their machinery or mechanized hog-raising operations. This visible recent trend, however, obscures a gradual and more fundamental change spanning several generations: farmers' adoption of the circular form for buildings and structures. If farmers of the 1880s could return to view the farm of the 1980s, many, if not most, structures would appear to them strange and bewildering. They would find their familiar nineteenth century cluster of small rectangular buildings broken up and softened by infusions of circular buildings and structures — from silos to slurry tanks, from grain bins and feed-mixing bins to corn cribs and water tanks. Among the earliest, and certainly the most spectacular, agricultural uses found for the circular form came when farmers introduced the round barn to the farm.

Iowa is actually a treasure trove for those searching for round barns. Our survey found that of 160 barns identified, 127 still stand. Although scattered throughout the state (nearly two-thirds of Iowa's 99 counties have at least one), there is a certain concentration in two groups along a line running from the southwest to the northeast corner of the state. Few other states have so many, partly because round barn construction seems to have confined itself largely to the midwestern dairy and Corn Belt states. We know, for example, that about 180 round barns have been identified in Wisconsin, 154 in Indiana, and 160 in Iowa, while Vermont reportedly had no more than 24, Michigan an estimated 25, and a search of Nebraska turned up but 36.[6] Yet, despite Iowa's comparatively large number and wide distribution of round barns, they remain uncommon: scarcely one-tenth of one percent of Iowa's 100,000 farms have one. Those that do have an architectural rarity as well as a striking reminder of an older style of farming.

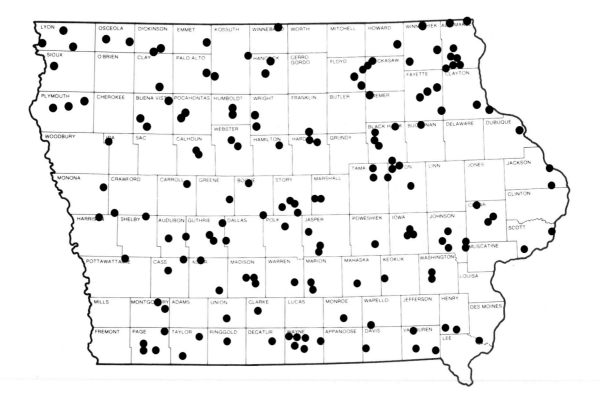

Relatively firm dates of construction could be determined for 93 of the 160 barns identified in this study. Taking these as a guide to building trends, the barns appeared during two periods in Iowa — the 1880s and the years between 1905 and 1920. Additional patterns emerge if this broad trend of construction is broken down into types of round barns: octagon, true-round, and other polygonal barns. Octagon barns completely dominated the first period, while true-round barns prevailed during the second. Other polygonal barns — the six, ten, twelve, and sixteen-sided varieties — could be found scattered throughout both periods, though most were built between 1910 and 1920. The story behind the trends reveals a significant aspect of the little-understood history of farm architecture.

Iowa Building Trends (1860-1930)

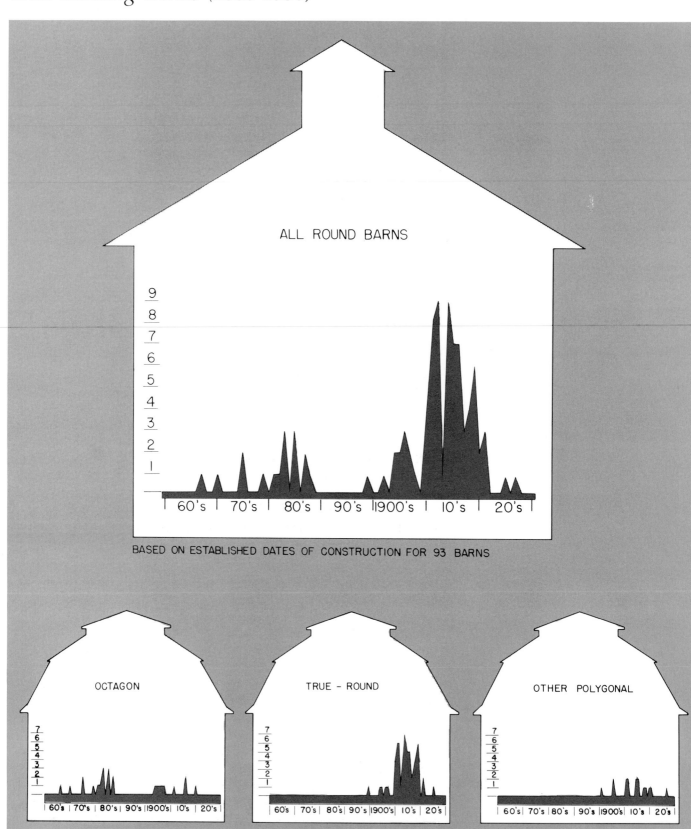

ALL ROUND BARNS

BASED ON ESTABLISHED DATES OF CONSTRUCTION FOR 93 BARNS

OCTAGON

TRUE - ROUND

OTHER POLYGONAL

The enthusiasm for building round barns in Iowa coincided with two surges of general barn building.[7] One wave of barn construction in Iowa that peaked in the early 1890s overlapped a time of round barn popularity, and a second peak, occurring about 1910, came exactly when round barn construction hit full stride. The fortuitous correspondence between general barn construction and interest in the round barn may explain why the state has so many good examples of this unusual building.

Still, questions arise. Where did Iowa's farmers get their idea for round barns? Were some farmers more likely to build round barns than others? Did interest in building round barns shift from one region of the state to another? Did specialists or local contractors build them? How were round barns built, with what materials, and how arranged? Although conclusive answers may evade us, many clues survive.

Despite B. J. Diers' fresh enthusiasm in 1914 for the round barn as a progressive new development, such barns dated back forty-five years in Iowa. Elsewhere in the nation isolated examples of round barns existed even earlier, although not until the latter part of the nineteenth century did they really catch on. The early round barns typically stood on show-place farms, the farms of wealthy landowners who could afford to indulge their whims in costly architectural experiments. George Washington's sixteen-sided barn is the earliest recorded barn of this type. Washington designed and built it for his Dogue Run Farm in Fairfax County, Virginia, in 1793. He wanted a place to thresh grain indoors, and this type of barn had a large square threshing floor suitable for that purpose. Washington supervised the storage of half the grain personally, but when he left, his overseer proceeded to take the grain outside to thresh it, not thirty feet from the barn. A disappointed Washington took this as proof of "the almost impossibility of putting the overseers of this country out of the track they have been accustomed to walk in."[8]

Probably the most famous, and perhaps the first, of the true-round barns was the Shaker barn at Hancock, Massachusetts. The Shakers put up a massive barn in 1824, ninety feet in diameter with thirty-inch stone walls. In the center was a space fifty-five feet wide and thirty feet high to hold hay, while around its outer edge fifty-two cattle could feed. The original barn burned down, but the Shakers built another in 1865.[9] Although the barn achieved renown, especially after being rebuilt, it was obviously not for every farmer. Shaker barns, even rectangular ones, were famous as oddities, being far larger than the average farmer could afford.

Examples of the patrician farmer with his round barn can be drawn from early agricultural newspapers. In 1854 the *Cultivator and Country Gentleman* illustrated an octagon barn on the Maryland farm of George Calvert. It was a huge structure standing among other barns on the farm, each with a specific use.[10] But when the farm journal's editor touted the barn for its convenience in feeding and ease of cleaning, his claims drew the ire of a Keokuk, Iowa reader who corresponded under the name "Hawkeye." Hawkeye criticized the size of the stalls, the width of the alleys, and the proposition that the barn could be easily cleaned.[11] Despite the scorn he received in later issues, Hawkeye stuck to his position.[12] The practical Midwest farmer rejected such a barn as the extravagant foolishness of gentleman farmers.

While the personal fancy of some produced a few circular barns before the mid-1850s, the philosophical convictions of another man, Orson Squire Fowler, took round barn sentiment in a different direction. Fowler, A New York phrenologist, readied a campaign during the 1850s to publicize the octagon form generally as he had publicized his other interests which ranged from phrenology to sex and marriage to gravel wall construction. The perfect shape in nature, as far as Fowler was concerned, was the circle, but the octagon approached it and could be built more easily. Living in and using an octagon-shaped dwelling, Fowler believed, would change the character of man; children of the future would be more amiable if they grew up in octagon homes.

Fowler expressed these beliefs in *A Home for All* (1849-1854), which, though concerned with houses, included a chapter on barns and carriage houses. He offered no barn plans, but described an ideal barn as being a two-story building with a ramp to the second floor. Thus he envisioned the ideal set of farm buildings to be an octagon house and an octagon barn. Nothing else would be needed.[13]

Students of octagon construction tend to presume that because Fowler influenced many people to build octagon houses he must necessarily have figured largely in octagon barn construction as well. This is surely debatable, however. Fowler's brief discussion of the octagon barn may have introduced this shape of building to a wider spectrum of people than the wealthy landowner or radical thinker, and certainly his writings prompted hundreds of octagon residences to be built, especially in New York, between 1850 and 1860.[14] But, unlike octagon houses, no barns can be traced directly to him. Moreover, a hiatus of almost thirty years separates publication of *A Home for All* from the building of most of Iowa's octagon barns, and farm journals had ceased any mention of Fowler by the early 1860s. His cause, with respect to barn architecture at least, evidently died aborning.

The octagon barn attracted its first effective advocates after the mid-1870s. Without reference to Fowler, certain farm improvement proponents among progressive farmers, stock breeders, and agricultural editors began to take an interest in octagon barns. Such octagon barns multiplied during the 1880s. The movement evident-

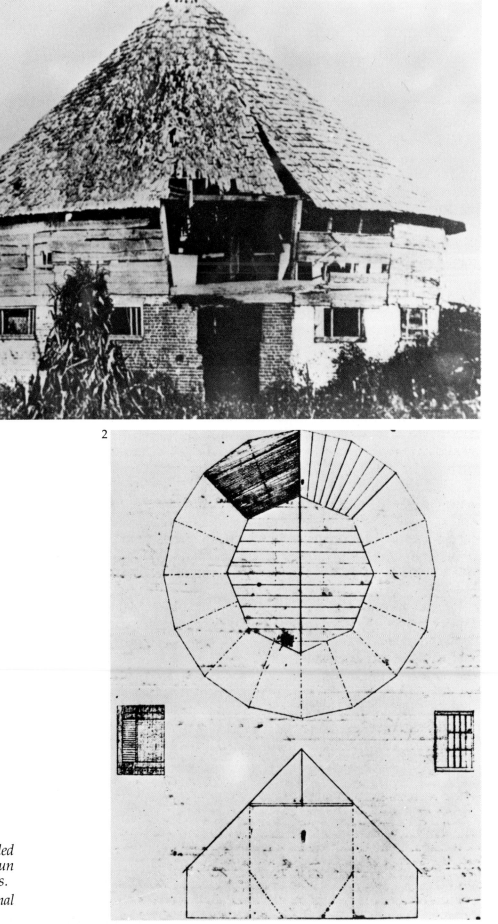

1

2

1. *George Washington's 16-sided barn (ca. 1895) at his Dogue Run farm. The barn no longer stands.*

2. *Part of Washington's original plan for the barn.*

ly owed its origins to Elliott W. Stewart at the national level and to Lorenzo S. Coffin in Iowa. Unlike Fowler, Stewart and Coffin were well known and respected agriculturalists who had personal experience with octagon barns and who also wrote for popular agricultural newspapers. Their promotional writings and the publicity given their examples, rather than any distant, indirect, or vague connections to Orson Fowler, inspired and largely explained Iowans' enthusiasm for octagon barns during these years. This generation, as we shall see, built most of the octagon barns we see today.

Chapter Two:

AN ERA OF OCTAGONS

Roberts barn, Sharon Center,
shown in a 1972 pencil drawing by
artist Marjorie B. Hayek.

In the summer of 1874, near Lake View in Erie County, New York, Elliott W. Stewart witnessed the burning of four rectangular barns on his farm. All these he replaced with a single new barn of octagon design. As he calculated it, the 5,350 square feet of space provided by his eighty-foot diameter octagon would be as useful as the total of 7,000 square feet of barn space contained in those destroyed. Stewart was no eccentric individualist who cared little about expounding upon his new barn's merits to others. Quite the contrary. As a farmer well-known in the state of New York, a lecturer on agriculture at Cornell University, and the editor of a farm journal, he made sure his views would be heard or read by large numbers of people. Enthusiastic about his summer's accomplishment, within three months Stewart had prepared a description, with engravings, of his barn for two winter issues of the monthly paper he edited, the Buffalo, *Live-Stock Journal*.[15] Reaction was immediate and favorable.

Readers began writing to the paper to obtain copies of his plan. Next, the editors of two leading agricultural journals, the *Cultivator and Country Gentleman* of Albany and the *American Agriculturalist* of New York City, took notice of it and reprinted it in their summer issues.[16] But interest did not end there, for the most popular source of Stewart's plan was yet to appear. The *Illustrated Annual Register of Rural Affairs* (published by the *Cultivator and Country Gentleman*) devoted a section of its 1878 volume to the "Construction of Barns," and included an expanded version of Stewart's article along with additional details by its author.[17] The introductory statement noted that barns of octagonal form "are now regarded with much favor by many intelligent agriculturalists." Another editor agreed. When in 1878 the *National Live-Stock Journal* of Chicago (successor to Stewart's Buffalo journal) reprinted Stewart's article of two years before, its editor noted the strong response still greeting the plan:

> So many applications were sent us for the numbers of that *Journal* containing these illustrations, that the large edition was soon exhausted; and as they continue to come in, in considerable numbers, even at this late day, we have thought best to reproduce the article, with the engravings.[18]

Two books followed, each of which featured Stewart's example. J. P. Sheldon's *Dairy Farming* described this "American Octagon Barn" to English dairymen as one "totally different from anything we are accustomed to in the way of farm buildings" but which "possesses certain valuable features" that make it worth trying.[19] In 1883, it also appeared as a segment in Elliott Stewart's new treatise entitled *Feeding Animals*, the publication of which solidified for him "a wide and enviable reputation" as a livestock management expert "both in this country and in England."[20] The octagon barn idea would indeed flourish.

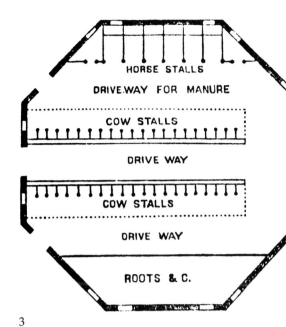

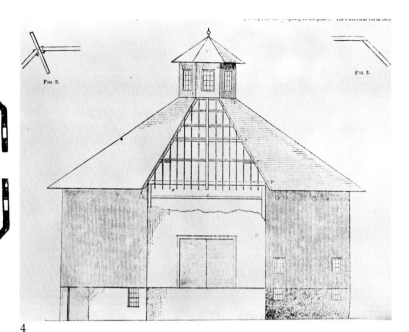

3

4

5

3. Main floor plan showing the interior arranged in a rectangular rather than circular fashion, which characterized barns of the 1880s.

4. Front elevation drawing of Stewart's barn first published in 1876.

5. Elliott W. Stewart, who created a fad for octagon barn construction during the 1880s, publicized his own example in various leading agricultural journals of the day. Stewart's barn and farm in Lake View, New York, no longer exist, having since been sold and subdivided as part of metropolitan suburban expansion in towns south of the City of Buffalo.

In 1884 a pleased Stewart noted his satisfaction not only with his own octagon barn but also with the fact that "some 30 or 40 have been built in various parts of the country — among them five in Pennsylvania, three in Indiana, four or five in Illinois, two in Minnesota, and several in Kentucky."[21] Throughout these years Stewart served as the expert on octagon barns for several nationally circulated farm papers. Progressive-minded farmers corrresponded with newspaper editors about octagon barn plans they had printed, debated the barns' advantages, and asked for specific information about how to adapt the plans to differing situations. Stewart handled the newspaper replies, most often responding to farmers' inquiries through *The Country Gentleman* and *Rural Affairs*.

Stewart saw the octagon barn as having major advantages over rectangular barns. First of all, the barns were cheaper to build. This was because a round or octagonal barn could, with fewer materials, contain more storage capacity than could a rectangular barn with walls of the same height. The true-round barn could hold even more than the octagon, acknowledged Professor Stewart, but he explained that "the true circle is too expensive to build and the octagon approaches the circle in economy of outside walls, and is as easily built as the square."[22] Second, the roof of his barn, being an octagonal cone, was very strong, and it had the advantage over rectangular barns of being self-supporting, that is, clear of any obstructing interior posts and purlins, so that a horse-drawn hay-fork might be run to any part. Stewart also gave other commonly cited reasons for the octagon's superiority over rectangular barns. "The octagon or sixteen-sided form," he said is much less affected by the wind, and may be built higher than the long barn in windy situations."[23] Also, Stewart insisted, for feeding purposes, "Barns that are square or circular have shorter lines of travel than the oblong form."[24] In an age when the farmer moved everything by hand inside his barn, convenience counted.

Arguing the octagon barn's merits on grounds of economy of construction, efficiency of use, and strength against winds, E. W. Stewart stood in the forefront of the expanding movement to improve farm practices.[25] And how did barns fit into efforts to promote better methods of farming? Unlike the trend in England, where two- and three-story multi-purpose farm buildings were becoming less popular than single-story buildings specially constructed for each farm purpose, the thrust of American interest was running in the opposite direction. "The American idea," reported J. P. Sheldon about 1880, "is to have the forage, cattle, and manure all under one roof" as a labor saving arrangement.[26] Byron D. Halstad further clarified this trend in *Barn Plans and Outbuildings* (1881) when he wrote:

> With the increase of wealth, and we may add of good sense and enlarged ideas, among the farmers of the country, there is a gradual but very decided improvement in farm architecture. The old custom was to build small barns, to add others on three sides of a yard, perhaps of several yards, and to construct sheds, pigpens, corn houses, and such minor structures as might seem desirable. Compared with a well arranged barn, a group of small buildings is inconvenient and extremely expensive to keep in good repair.[27]

"In constructing farm buildings," Halstad further observed, "the error is usually on the side of too small structures, as the thousands of lean-to sheds, 'annex' stables, and hay stacks, etc., through the country testify to."[28] Stewart helped lead the way. His octagon barn exemplified how a single barn could replace four other barns, and he voiced that belief in his claim: "This form of building, properly understood, would lead farmers to abandon the building of a separate barn for each specific purpose, and to providing for all their necessities under one roof."[29]

The same reasons moved an influential agriculturalist in Iowa, the pioneer stock breeder Lorenzo S. Coffin, to urge acceptance of the octagon barn. Although he did not begin, despite repeated requests, to publicize his own octagon barn until Stewart's broader campaign was well underway, the barn he built predated that of Elliott Stewart by eight years. Its 1867 vintage made it the earliest known octagon barn in the state. On Willow Edge, his farm near Fort Dodge, Coffin hewed framing timber and shingle shakes from his nearby woods and transported additional lumber forty miles by wagon to build a sixty-eight-foot octagon barn. Coffin raised blooded livestock, and the octagon barn was part of his model farm.[30] If his, or for that matter Elliott Stewart's, inspiration for the octagon barn came from reading either Fowler's book or articles about the Calvert barn in 1854, or came independently from working as an experiment-minded patrician farmer, neither man said. During the early 1870s an occasional Iowa farmer built a small octagonal barn, probably for the family horse and carriage, but it was the publicity of Stewart's and Coffin's examples that evidently inspired two varieties of larger eight-sided barns erected in Iowa during the 1880s.[31]

6. *Lorenzo S. Coffin (1888 engraving), one of Iowa's leading agricultural improvement spokesmen of his day.*

7. *Coffin's octagon barn as it looked in 1959, about a decade before its collapse.*

8. *Early octagon barns in Iowa tended to be small in size like this barn on the Jno. F. Hopkin's farmstead at the south edge of Madrid in 1875.*

6

7

8

9

The barn designs of Stewart and Coffin differed most fundamentally at two points: in their design for entries to lower and upper levels and in the type of roof adopted. Stewart's bank-type barn lacked the ease of entry to the second, or "loft", level that Coffin's possessed, because the lower story began at ground level, and earth had to be graded up at a considerable incline to form a "bank" driveway to the second floor. Coffin, on the other hand, built his barn with the basement sunk in a natural or excavated depression in the land so that, without difficulty, horses could draw their loads into the barn at nearly ground level by either crossing a ramp to the hillside upper story or driving into the basement entry at the base of the hill. But whatever inferiority Stewart's barn showed in providing for easy entry, it made up for in the superiority of his roof design.

Stated simply, Stewart's barn had a self-supporting roof and Coffin's did not. With a self-supporting roof such as Stewart's rigid octagonal or pyramidal cone, in which eight wedge-shaped sections met together at the center, the loft space was clear, without the intrusion of supporting posts or purlins. Coffin's roof of modified hip design, however, could not do without these obstructions,

9. The latticework of supporting posts and braces in modified hip roof barns made them more difficult to fill with hay.

10. In contrast, a barn constructed with a self-supported 8-section cone roof gave a loft of unrestricted open space.

10

which got in the way when filling the loft with hay and grain. Octagon barn carpenters built a roof of Coffin's type by extending four large trapezoidal sections directly to the top and fitting four smaller sections into the remaining triangular spaces. Since it was not a clear span, in which the entire roof load could rest on the walls of the barn, part of the load at the roof's "hip" midpoint had to be transmitted to the ground through inside posts.

If the differences between these two features are clues showing to whom Iowa farmers turned for their basic barn design, they reveal a story of split influence. Of thirteen identified octagon barns evidently built between 1878 and 1890, the roof types of five were of the octagonal cone type, like Stewart's, six were of Coffin's modified hip design, and two resembled neither. Only three of the five with Stewart's roof type, however, followed his idea of a full above-ground basement with steep inclined driveway to the second floor. Four of the six farmers using Coffin's modified hip roof joined him in placing the basement in a depression of the ground or into the slope of a hill.

Among octagons in Iowa that resemble Stewart's barn, at least in roof form, perhaps the earliest one was Philander Thompson's southwest of Clarinda in Page County.[32] Erected in the early 1880s, the magnificent fifty-six-foot diameter barn stood as a landmark in the area and was visible from several miles around until the late 1950s when, after the roof caved in, the owner removed the barn walls. He then put a roof over the foundation and now uses it for

11

12

hog confinement. Perhaps the first duplicate of Coffin's design came in the late 1870s. George Davenport, a farmer near Delta, Iowa, saw a similar structure when he visited relatives in Greene County, and he came back home with all the necessary specifications.[33] What he had seen, in all probability, was Coffin's barn in adjoining Webster County. Davenport proceeded to haul rock for a foundation from a site two miles away and, with a four-horse team, dragged the necessary white pine timber by bobsled from Washington, Iowa. When completed, the "split entry" octagon barn ultimately served him and succeeding owners for nearly the next ninety years. But finally in 1964 its owner needed a more convenient building and the octagon barn, judged to have too much "cold" and "useless" space, ceased being a landmark on the Keokuk County landscape.[34]

These scattered instances of early construction bespoke growing interest, but it was in 1883 that octagon barn prospects in Iowa got their greatest boost. Lorenzo Coffin, then one of the state's leading farm editors, for the Fort Dodge *Messenger*, and Benjamin F. Gue, editor of the state's leading agricultural paper, the *Iowa Homestead*, joined in inaugurating the chain of events. In an October 1882 issue, the *Homestead's* editor excerpted one of Coffin's "Home and Farm" columns in which he extolled the advantages of octagon barns. Duly impressed, editor Gue then arranged for Coffin to prepare a lengthy article giving a full description of his own 1867 octagon barn. The editor made this his front-page story in the lead

January issue of 1883. The paper's wood engraver presented cuts illustrating the barn and its layout so that, as Gue put it, "any good builder" could "readily duplicate this fine barn".[35]

"It has been a wonder to me," Coffin wrote in his piece, "that this form of barn has not become more common. Everything is in its favor — economy, convenience and safety." Despite its "immense" storage capacity, Coffin believed that the fact that "only a small part of the octagon barn is square against any wind," explained why "the hardest winds we have had here since it was built hardly make it tremble." Although some might imagine the roof "would be hard to frame," Coffin assured his readers that it was "very simple." In fact, builders ought not be reluctant to erect a barn of this shape generally, he thought, for it "is as easily framed as a rectangular one." Writing from an experience of fourteen years with an octagon barn, Coffin could firmly attest that "we like it better and better every year."[36]

Several subscribers immediately requested specifications on the lumber used and the cost of the barn.[37] Others, however, were not so sure and gave respectful, but mixed, reactions. One reader "admired very much the plan of Mr. Coffin's barn," but then went on to suggest that "as so few of us can find the money to build such a barn, its well to discuss the more commonly raised shed and stable question."[38] Another, promoting his own rectangular barn design argued that "an octagon barn is more complicated than a hexagonal one, and a hexagonal one more complicated than a rectangular one; while a rectangular barn like mine can be constructed by any farmer at no expense except for lumber and hardware and his own labor."[39]

13

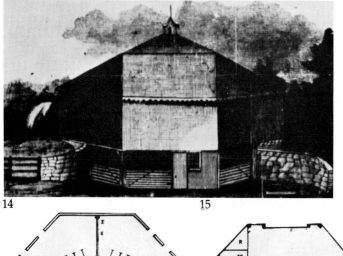

14   15

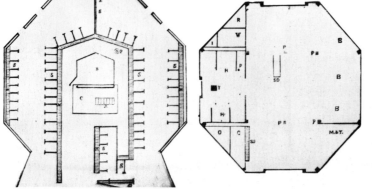

13. Woodcut of Lorenzo S. Coffin's 1867 octagon barn published in 1883 by the Des Moines Iowa Homestead. *It shows the main entry to the lower level of the east facade and access to the upper level from a rise in the hillside to the left.*

14. Basement floor plan.

15. Upper level floor plan.

Two 1883 octagons closely resembled and followed on the heels of publicity about Lorenzo Coffin's barn:

16. John Roberts barn in Johnson County.

17. Jasper Township barn in Carroll County.

19

17

Despite the doubts of some, those Iowans who had the means and were not intimidated by the octagon's seemingly more complicated and unfamiliar design began to erect these experimental barns. At least two appeared in 1883 that bore striking similarities to Coffin's barn — one northeast of Carroll in Carroll County and another on John Roberts' farm southwest of Iowa City in Johnson County. Each, like Coffin's, was a ramp barn built into a depression in the land so that its owners could enter the basement on ground level and also drive into the floor above nearly on a level with the ground. Both shared Coffin's roof and heavy timber framing of Coffin's design and, with slight variations, the same dimensions. The interior layout of the Carroll County barn resembled Coffin's, but John Roberts' version in Johnson County eliminated the upper-level horse stalls, substituting instead storage area for additional hay and oats.[40]

Meanwhile, Joshua H. Secrest, a prosperous farmer just west of Downey in Johnson County proceeded that spring to construct on his 520-acre homestead an octagon barn of even more radical design. Its innovative framing and large size equalled Secrest's aspirations and enhanced local reputation for progressive farming. The editor of a nearby West Branch newspaper proclaimed that the barn, when completed, "will be the largest building of the kind in the country," containing "stable room for thirty-two horses and sixteen cows, room for two hundred tons of hay, and furnished with all the modern improvements."[41]

18. Octagon barn and farmstead of Joshua H. Secrest, near Downey, in an 1893 engraving.

19. Graceful lines and structural sophistication mark the Secrest octagon barn in its exterior appearance.

20. Eighteen 1 × 6-inch strips of wood went into building each laminated beam.

21. A large unobstructed loft was achieved by laminated beam construction.

18

23

22. The date of construction for this Story County octagon barn is unknown. But the modified hip-roof form, heavy timber frame construction, and non-circular interior arrangement mark the barn as one built in the 1880s along lines suggested in the publicized plan of Lorenzo S. Coffin's barn in Webster County.

23. Stone foundations characterize nearly all octagon barns built during the era of the 1880s. Thereafter, concrete assumed almost complete dominance.

More remarkable than its size was the barn's structural sophistication. George Frank Longerbeam, the master builder whom Secrest commissioned to erect the barn, eliminated the usual heavy timber posts rising up from within to support the roof at its midpoint. This he achieved by constructing hand-laminated forty-foot-long beams from 1 × 6 inch strips (18 per beam) that he soaked, curved, and fastened together. The result: a majestic group of gently curved beams that stretched from the base of the loft to the roof's apex in support of a graceful bell-shaped roof hovering over an immense interior space. These features make the barn an outstanding example of early rural architecture that in 1974 qualified it for entry in the National Register of Historic Places.[42]

Enthusiasm for octagon barns continued in Iowa. At least six more octagons appeared during the remaining seven years of the 1880s. The evident success of the Secrest barn, for instance, prompted Longerbeam to repeat his plan in the immediate neighborhood. This second barn, also with a laminated frame and bell-shaped roof, is somewhat smaller and presently stands within one and one-half miles of its predecessor, alone in the middle of a field. Both barns are visible to travelers on Highway 6 just east of Iowa City. A Guthrie County farmer also erected an octagon barn on his farm in Richland Township. In 1887 another went up in the northwest corner of Bremer County in eastern Iowa. Another builder constructed two others in nearby Fayette County in the late 1880s. These barns were identical but for their fates — only one survives today. Three undated barns may also belong to the same period; they are similar in construction, interior arrangement and general appearance to the dated barns. Two, resembling Lorenzo Coffin's barn, are located in Story County in central Iowa and Winneshiek County in the northeast; a third, with a roof composed of pie-shaped sections like that of Elliott Stewart's design, is in Lyon County to the northwest.[43]

Little is known of the individuals who actually constructed octagons during these years. Owners may have found plans and then looked for an experienced carpenter to carry them out, or perhaps some builder specializing in octagon barns convinced farmers to build in that style, as a barn builder did in Wisconsin.[44] There is, nevertheless, a great deal of similarity among most of these barns of the 1880s regardless of who built them. Erected on foundations of stone, the octagons were of heavy timber construction, i.e., mortise and tenon and wooden pegs rather than nails, or else a combination of heavy timber and nailed frame construction (these were the techniques common to all barns of the period). Vertical board and batten siding most often covered the frame. Most were split entry barns with a bank or ramp to an upper level for storage and ground-floor doors on the lower level for the animals. Originally each had an octagon cupola, although two extant barns have subsequently lost theirs.

The arrangement of interior space in a rectangular rather than circular fashion further distinguished this era of octagon barns. Part of the reason for rectangular interiors no doubt stemmed from the prevailing construction system of interior posts and braces for handling roof loads that made a circular plan awkward and inconvenient. But, more important, the circular plan (which characterized later round barns) made little sense to farmers in the 1880s. Octagon barns predated the use of cylindrical silos, which, would later encourage many farmers to see that more efficient use of interior space could result by arranging stalls and runways around a central silo. Until that happened considerations of efficiency suggested that stalls be situated on each side of a driveway running through the barn's center. There was a great waste of space in a circular plan, E. W. Stewart concluded in 1878, because a circular driveway running around the barn's interior wall would consume over three times as much space as driveways running before and behind straight rows of cow stalls.[45] Even when farmers began thinking about building a silo in the center of the barn, the difficulty of filling it led most to await the introduction of on-the-farm elevator devices for lifting the silage.[46]

Surprisingly, four barns of the period for which individual builders are known depart from the typical style. The two barns built east of Iowa City by Longerbeam achieved a clear span interior loft by the unconventional use of laminated beams. There is another variation in the two barns built in Fayette County. When Joe Butler, a West Union carpenter, built an octagon barn on the Patterson farm in the late 1880s, he constructed a roof like Stewart's octagonal cone (without cupola) but added a hay dormer to it on one side to make the loft easier to fill with grain. This feature, ahead of its time in such barns, answered charges that octagonal barns were hard to fill with hay. After its construction a nearby farmer, M. W. Grimes, came to Butler and asked for the same barn. The builder obliged and soon an identical barn stood three miles away. The Grimes barn subsequently had a milk room added on its south side. Although the Patterson barn no longer exists, the Grimes barn remains.

The dispersed location of these 1880s barns raises questions about what kind of farmer built them, for no pronounced clustering or regional pattern is visible today.[47] The barns were not generally in the western part of the state, the part most recently settled. But they were not necessarily in the oldest part of the state either. Also, octagon barn owners of the 1880s did not appear to share a special interest, such as building their barns for a specific use beyond that of general farm purposes. Concerns about wind damage may have prompted many of these prairie farmers to build octagon and round barns. Contemporary statements and oral tradition to that effect abound in published and other sources. An Iowa subscriber to *Breeder's Gazette,* for example, wrote in 1902 to obain a round barn plan because, explained the editor, "in his neighborhood nearly all the barns have been destroyed by wind storms and he wants something that will not blow away."[48] The Lewis Clark round barn in Monroe County is made up of old timber from rectangular barns that had blown down. Most likely the octagon barn's popularity in the 1880s derived from such concerns coinciding with publicity on barn examples in popular agricultural journals. The design of a farmer's octagon barn emulated these newsworthy examples, with variations according to the predilections of the farmer and those of his builder.

Chapter Three:

"SILO BARNS" ECLIPSE RIVALS

Miller barn, Riverside, featured in a 1970 pencil drawing by Marjorie B. Hayek.

As the octagon barn's popularity began to wane by 1890, advancing technical knowledge was laying the groundwork for a new type — the true-round, silo-shaped barn. It was a type that, unlike its octagon forebears, proved to be an outgrowth of engineering research rather than the experience of local carpenters. Earlier, prevailing construction techniques had favored the octagon shape over the true circle as being easier and less expensive to build. But now three unconnected developments gradually made it possible to reverse this emphasis. First, with increased frequency barn builders substituted light-dimension "balloon framing" for that of traditional heavy timber framing. Balloon frame construction was cheaper and required less skill, and the system's elasticity made possible both endless new shapes and sizes of buildings and new, more efficient interior arrangements beyond those imposed by the old post and beam method. Second, the successful development of a properly constructed, large, self-supporting roof for true-round barns left the loft space unobstructed for storage. Finally, the introduction of the circular silo as a replacement for octagon, square, and other early silos made building-in-the-round a more familiar and accepted feature of farm construction. This latter achievement merits discussion at the outset.

That both the true-round barn and the circular silo gained popularity almost simultaneously was no mere coincidence, for it was Franklin H. King, a physics professor at the Wisconsin Agricultural Experiment Station at Madison, who carried out the initial engineering research into both kinds of structures. By the late 1880s, with about a decade of silo building experience to draw on, King was engaged in a study of silos then in use, with a view to "suggesting remedies" for their many "serious imperfections" in construction. When published in 1891, his important findings would give persuasive strength to the case for adopting cylindrical silos and for building what became known as the Wisconsin or King all-wood silo.[49] But in early 1889 he was also busy with another task — designing the first of what was to become a generation of true-cylindrical barns.

King's brother, who farmed near Whitewater, Wisconsin, had written a letter to Franklin requesting that he design a barn to enclose eighty cows and ten horses economically under one roof with feeding and cleaning alleys before and behind, plus a silo, a granary, and sufficient storage space for dry fodder. Professor King considered the usual styles of barn architecture to be impractical for meeting these needs and devised a circular plan as an alternative. Soon, during the spring of 1889, a local builder was at work erecting it on the C. E. King farm.[50]

24. *The cylindrical barn designed by King for his brother's farm near Whitewater, Wisconsin, featured main entrances to the first and second stories.*

25. *Professor Franklin H. King (ca. 1909) originated the post-1890 generation of true-round barns.*

26. *Cutaway drawing shows King's marriage of his silo design with a balloon-frame barn.*

24

25

26

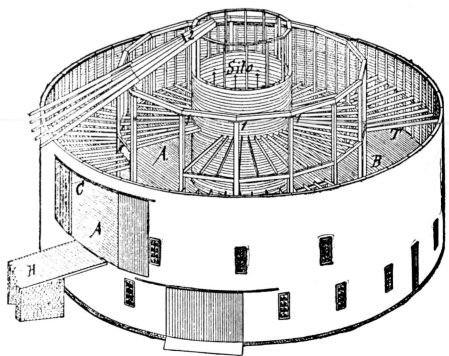

The barn's all wood construction features amounted to a gigantic, ninety-two-foot diameter version of what was soon to be King's recommended round silo, right down to its horizontal siding. In all likelihood, King also became the first designer to put a silo in the center of the barn — a characteristic arrangement of twentieth century round barns. Except for the fact that it lacked a self-supporting roof, the barn's balloon frame construction and circular layout surrounding a central silo made it a prototype of what was to come.

King published the plan, with explanation, in the 1890 *Annual Report* of the Wisconsin Agricultural Experiment Station as one "believed to be worthy of general imitation."[51] W. D. Hoard reprinted it in an 1895 issue of his farm paper, *Hoard's Dairyman*. When, in 1897, a farmer built another such barn in Amsterdam, New York, along lines suggested by King, the editor once again publicized the event. He devoted substantial front-page space to a story about it (including photos and ground-floor plans) written by King for the paper's March 26 issue.[52] J. H. Sanders reprinted King's original plan in his *Practical Hints About Farm Building* in 1893, as did the Chicago *Breeder's Gazette* in both its weekly journal and in editions of its book, *Farm Buildings*. And, of course, King himself included it in all six editions of his popular textbook on agriculture.[53]

The Illinois experiment station next picked up the true-round barn and improved upon it. Between 1900 and 1910, H. E. Crouch of the Dairy Department planned and supervised the construction of three round barns on the campus at Champaign, Illinois. The barns reflected improvements that promised to bring round barns into more general use. They made more provision for light and sunshine — a deficiency in King's barns. But most important, they incorporated the self-supporting roof as an integral and necessary element of round barn design. This eliminated the need for a structure of interior posts to handle the load of a supported roof. Although self-supporting roofs had been in use on some round barns before this time, the Illinois advocates focused on the necessity of such a roof if the round barn's full potential were to be realized. Crouch, in 1914, put the achievement in perspective:

> Professor King was entirely right in his argument for the round barn and to him is due the honor of introducing this valuable type of barn into this country. It was left for other men, however, to develop a type of construction that was economical and practical. The chief factor which kept the King type of barn from being popular was not its shape, but its construction. At the present time there are four types of roofs for circular barns that are far superior to the King type, all of which are self-supporting and require no scaffolding for their erection.[54]

The Illinois station presented plans and detailed instructions in an experiment station bulletin in 1910 and again in a revised edition in 1918. Widely circulated, these publications lent authoritative support to the round barn as a legitimate type of farm architecture worthy of adoption. Upon its publication, the first bulletin created "considerable comment," reported Henry A. Wallace of *Wallaces' Farmer*. "The facts presented in it were so convincing," he pointed out to his readers, "that it was difficult to see how anyone could think of building a dairy barn other than a round one."[55] The surge

27. *Three true-round barns built at the University of Illinois, Urbana, which the agricultural experiment station publicized in publications issued 1910 and 1918, spurred others in Iowa and elsewhere to be erected during those years.*

28. *"The term 'self supporting roof' is a misnomer in a way," pointed out agriculturalist Herbert Shearer in 1917, because the central silo often supported it at the top. This extra prop, he advised, was the best approach. Evidently, Shearer and others did not yet accept builders' claims that the self-supported roof was "plenty stiff enough to withstand the strongest winds without any support other than the round shell of the building itself."*

of true-round barn construction that occurred after 1910 was due in large part to the work and publicity of the Illinois Experiment Station.

The final major circular barn innovation — replacing wooden walls with walls of vitrified clay tile — evidently originated in Iowa as an elaboration of the Illinois designs. Silo experiments again provided the idea. In 1908 Professor J. B. Davidson and Matt King of the Iowa Experiment Station at Ames, working with a local tile manufacturer, had pioneered the use of clay tile in a round silo.[56] The engineers first used rectangular drain tile for the wall of the silo and then encouraged the local tile works to make hollow curved tile. Once achieved, the curved clay tile gave Ames station engineers the means to suggest a plan for a round clay-tile barn.[57] The plan described a round barn sixty feet in diameter with a sixteen by forty-six-foot silo in the center and a ten-by-fifteen foot water tank on top. (The experiment station researchers had found that the hollow-tile water tanks gave excellent results if properly constructed.)[58] It also called for a concrete floor, clay block walls for the hay floor, and a self-supporting roof. The interior arrangement showed a circle of thirty-six stalls facing in, two drives to a second floor, and a dairy room underneath. This type of barn, sixty feet in diameter and two stories high, became known locally as the "Iowa barn."

29.   *Cross section drawing shows the water tank within a silo that Ames agricultural experiment station engineers had perfected. The floor plan was characteristic of those adopted for Iowa clay-tile barns.*

30.   *Roof construction in progress.*

31.   *The completed barn.*

29

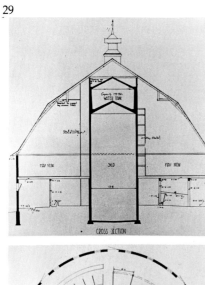

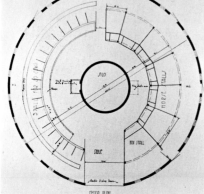

30

These new developments at the Wisconsin, Illinois, and Iowa experiment stations influenced what was built by Iowa's progressive farmers. During the prosperous years before and during the First World War, many updated their operations by adding to or replacing buildings constructed twenty to thirty years earlier. And in the progressive spirit of experimentation, circular and polygonal barns enjoyed a second boom in popularity that not only rivaled but far exceeded that of the 1880s.

Of the 127 true-round and polygonal barns still standing in Iowa, nine out of ten were built (or are estimated to have been built) after 1890. True-round barns comprise nearly three-fourths of that total. Despite the decided trend toward building true-round barns, a few farmers continued to put up octagon barns, but now they used only octagonal cone roofs instead of Coffin's inferior hip-roof design. During the transition to strictly round barns, several farmers used plans for twelve- to sixteen-sided barns, and a few others devised their own versions: the six, nine, ten, eleven, and thirteen-and-one-half-sided barns.

Aside from their obvious difference in shape, four features distinguished the true-round barn generation from its older octagon forebears. First and foremost, the interior space was arranged differently. Interiors of octagons had been arranged the same as rectangular barns. True-round barn plans, on the other hand, called

31

for mangers, feeding and cleaning alleys, box stalls, and other functions to be arranged in a circle, usually around a centrally placed silo. Second, the self-supported roof completely supplanted the older hip-roof design. Third, new materials characterized the post-1890 true-round barns. Curved vitrified clay tile assumed decided leadership in farmer acceptance over all-wood construction even though wood barns more easily accommodated later additions. A few farmers sided their round barns with sheet or corrugated metal, while others tried concrete, which was being used with increasing frequency on the farm. Several extant barns have walls of either poured concrete, cement blocks, or concrete staves. Last, barn uses became more specialized. Strictly dairy barns appeared more often, as did barns that held special registered stock. Others served as farm sales barns for marketing rather than for raising and housing animals.

32

33

34

32-33. Inside a working silo barn. A Mennonite family — still using horses — keeps the barn clean and well-maintained in full original use as a dairy barn in Buchanan County.

34. Many old styles of silos that tell the story of the silo's early development are still found protected within round barns. The once-common wood stave silo, shown here in a Winneshiek County barn, is today among the seldom seen.

35. A rare King/Gurler silo (wood stave lined with a layer of cement or plaster for durability) was within the Tonsfeldt round barn in Plymouth County.

36. Wood true-round barns varied in their exterior finish. Certainly farmers painted the barns different colors — red, white, or yellow — or left them to weather unpainted, as in this abandoned Allamakee County barn. Besides the differences in color, variety extended to siding. The wood siding might be put on vertically using boards and batten, or, as shown here, with sawed lumber — the board without the batten. Horizontally-applied siding distinguished several other round barns, but vertical wood siding proved most common and stood the years better.

37

37. *Round barns with walls constructed of cement staves are close relatives to the silo. As with silos, metal hoops hold the staves in place. Pictured here is one of two such barns in Madison County.*

38. *Clay-tile barns ordinarily had few additions beyond a small milk room. But here a Tama County farmer added a long, wide rectangular ell that went far toward absorbing much of its original round shape.*

39. *Frank Silver's sales pavilion, built for his huge Hampshire hog operation, sported plenty of dormers in the loft to light the several guest rooms located there.*

38

The best example of a sales arena on a specialized livestock farm is the Wickfield barn near Cantril. This barn has three stories and a basement. The basement served as a dining room for the patrons of the sales, while the first floor contained the sales ring itself. Here the auctioneer sold prize Hampshire hogs raised on what was claimed to be the largest Hampshire hog farm in the world. The second floor had eight guest bedrooms and the third floor held a dance hall, a social club for drinking, and card room. Rumor has it that the barn became a private club or speakeasy during Prohibition. It is now used for little but storage.

Few of the twenty-nine wood true-round barns located in the state could be traced directly back to the prototype designs of either Franklin King or of researchers at the Illinois Experiment Station. Yet the influence of these men, in a derivative way, seems clear. The purely conical type of roof found in King's plan, for example, characterized four of the five true-round barns known to have been built in Iowa before the Illinois Experiment Station issued its bulletin in 1910. Thereafter, the pattern was reversed, and nearly two out of three owners of true-round barns chose to use the recommended gambrel type of self-supporting roof. Another indicator of close lineage is seen in Charles B. Reynolds' barn in Lyon County Iowa.

Reynolds built a true-round barn during the summer of 1904 that was subsequently featured as "An Iowa Round Barn" in the 1905 issue of the Chicago *Breeder's Gazette* and in successive editions of their popular book called *Farm Buildings*.[59] To all exterior appearances, the conical roof form and horizontal siding of Reynolds' barn emulated Franklin King's circular barn design. He was aware of King's ideas; when he wrote to the *Breeder's Gazette* about a round barn he visited in northern Illinois a month or two after completing his own barn, he noted its similarity to the plan found in King's *Physics of Agriculture*[60]. But Reynolds' fund of available round-barn knowledge and experience was by 1904 not limited simply to King's writings. Being a reader of *Breeder's Gazette*, Reynolds no doubt had already seen the paper's 1902 story portraying a Warren County, Indiana, round barn as well as the 1903 issue that featured a large circular cattle barn in nearby South Dakota. Perhaps these impelled him, after installing part of the foundation for his seventy-foot barn, to write Joseph E. Wing, the *Breeder's Gazette's* farm buildings specialist, to learn of his ideas. Wing, believing that the seventy-foot diameter barn would "not divide up satisfactorily into stalls in a circle," recommended instead a rectangular arrangement with "the idea being to arrange the posts so that they would be in the partitions and not in the way."[61] This, with but one change which left a part undivided and open for sheep, Reynolds adopted. It made the overall resulting plan one with features traceable to King, Wing, and Reynolds himself.

Reynolds soon regretted having neither made the side walls higher nor having installed windows over the big doors to let in "more light on dark winter days when the door must be kept shut," but within a few years an even bigger mistake became apparent. The straight conical roof that he had designed to be somehow self-supporting — "there being," as he said, "no posts or obstructions in the mow" — did not work out.[62] With its weak point being near the unsupported center where the lower and upper rafters met, and with the strong downward pull at this point whenever Reynolds used his slack rope carrier to lift heavy loads of hay into the mow, it is hardly surprising that a stronger two-pitch gambrel type self-supporting roof had to eventually replace this flawed predecessor.[63]

40. *Charles B. Reynolds' true-round barn in Lyon County, as originally built in 1904, illustrated the consequences of King's inferior type of straight conical roof. Here the problem was magnified, both because the cone roof lacked the amount of loft storage space found in a self-supported gambrel roof and because Reynolds failed to see the need for supports at the roof's midpoint so that the original had to be replaced eventually with a new two-pitch gambrel roof.*

41. *Barn as it looks today.*

40

41

The Illinois plans clearly prompted the construction of at least one Iowa barn, built on the Frantz farm in Greene County. "It was my mother," wrote Haven W. Frantz in 1976, "who told me of the interesting story of its building. According to her, the plans were drawn up one night around the kitchen table by my father and a local contractor, Beecher Lamb. All they had to go on were some ideas they got from an old U.S.D.A. bulletin from 1910."[64] Together they altered them for Frantz's specific needs, substituting, for example, exterior walls of concrete block for those of wood. In the summer of 1911 they put up the barn. Illustrative of how information about the round barns might spread, five years later a photograph and description of the completed barn appeared in *Farm Buildings: How to Build Them*, published by W. E. Frudden of Charles City. This book in turn went out to still more contractors and farmers. So those who had not seen the original Illinois bulletin might still have been exposed to the same general plans.

As for the clay-tile round "Iowa barn" — the single most common choice — most in the state show a general similarity to the Ames plan, usually being sixty feet in diameter in accordance with the specifications, although none matched the description in all particulars.[65] A barn built near Mason City in 1912 (see illustration), was described by its builder as having an "Iowa silo" along with the recommended hollow-tile water tank on top, which he said "has been experimented on for the past few years by the Iowa Experiment Station."[66] At the same time, his plan failed to incorporate the Ames recommendation for two drives to the second floor and a dairy room underneath. Notwithstanding the farmers' ubiquitous variations from the general design, the ideas on hollow-clay-tile round barns that originated from the Ames station acted as an undeniable catalyst for such construction. This is demonstrated in noting that more than one-half of the true-round barns built after 1890 are of hollow-clay-tile construction, and all of them went up after 1910, when the Iowa experiment station, in collaboration with local clay-tile manufacturers, circulated its plans. Clay tile steadily increased its share of the total.

The clay-tile barns in Iowa tended to be located in different areas from true-round wooden barns, even though the two styles were popular at the same time.[67] The preponderance of round clay-tile barns appeared in the northern half of the state: thirty-one of thirty-eight being north of present Interstate Highway 80. The less costly wooden barns appeared more often in less wealthy parts of the state: in southern Iowa (where few clay-tile works existed) and in the northeastern counties (where wood was plentiful). Allamakee County, for example, has five true-round barns and one twelve-sided wooden barn, but none of clay tile.

Farmers and carpenters had undoubtedly drawn upon published plans for their basic design information, but then made endless variations on them. Not one barn in Iowa precisely duplicated another. As one might expect, interior arrangements varied the most, because every farmer — depending on his desires and the kind and size of his holdings, his machinery, and other farm outbuildings — had a slightly different use in mind for his barn's

42. Henry A. Frantz, of Greene County, built his barn in 1911 based on a plan from the Illinois Agricultural Experiment Station, Bulletin 143. Here, in the fall of 1912, Frantz (seated on his steam engine) is working to fill the silo inside. A belt stretches out from around the steam engine's high pulley wheel to clear the incline and power a silage cutter located inside. The loads of fodder had to be hauled up the incline to the cutter.

interior spaces. Personal preferences for interiors notwithstanding, the farmer also had plenty to choose from in matters of exterior design. He could select from among the mix of roof shapes, cupolas, basement or ground-level entries, window and door openings, dormers, and various types of wood or masonry walls. Take roof designs, for instance. As the nearby figure illustrates, roofs of eleven shapes and sizes presented themselves to the farm owner. The one he chose depended on how his wishes matched the skills and imagination of his available carpenter-builder. Finally, as discussed earlier, the farmer found his selection partly dictated by the conventional wisdom about how to construct such barns at the time he decided to build one.

While it is useful to know how ideas for octagon and true-round barns originated and spread in Iowa, this is only part of the story. The movement's dynamic — the ebb and flow of arguments persuading farmers to accept or reject the form — is more fully revealed in the attempt to popularize true-round barns and in the controversy that surrounded it.

Round barn design from Louden Barn Plans *(Fairfield, Iowa: Louden Machinery Co., 1915), p. 38.*

Basic Roof Shapes

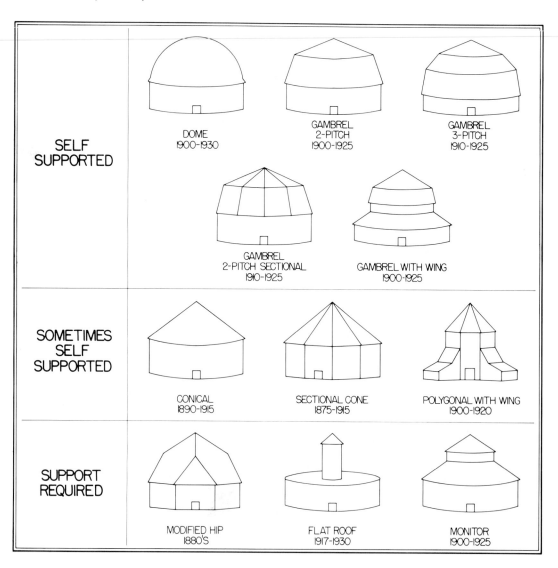

Design 4002 — For 32 Cows

Description

This barn is 60 ft. in outside diameter.

The foundation wall extends 30 inches above the ground and the frame side walls are 20 ft. high.

The lower story is 8 ft. high, the hay mow is 22 ft. high from floor to carrier track, the vertical side walls in the hay mow are 13 ft. high and the top of roof (not including ventilator cupola) is 40 ft. above the ground.

Mow capacity, 95 tons loose hay.

The foundation wall, lower floor and silo foundation are of concrete construction, balance of barn is of plank-frame construction.

The cost is estimated to be $2,800.00.

Cost does not include silo nor approach and bridge to hay mow floor.

This barn has the same capacity for live stock, feed and hay storage as the rectangular barn shown on page 39. The round barn covers a ground area of 2,827 square feet which is 651 sq. ft. more than required for the rectangular barn of same capacity.

This round barn also requires more feet of track for overhead carriers and all equipment costs more than in rectangular barn because it must be made to special curves.

Curved cement manger construction is also more expensive to build than straight construction.

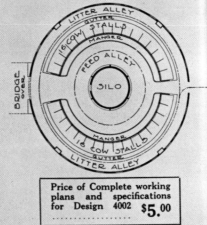

Price of Complete working plans and specifications for Design 4002 **$5.**00

Chapter Four:

SPREADING THE GOSPEL

Unlike barn construction efforts during the era of octagons, the push for true-round and polygonal barn construction after 1900 often took the shape of an organized commercial enterprise, less reliant on the haphazard efforts of agricultural newspaper editors and wealthy experimental farmer publicists. Inspired by the authoritative backing for round barns given in experiment station research publications, a new breed of barn specialist moved into the field — farm plan services, individual contractors, architects, and companies supplying the actual barn precut at the factory. Such specialists, often using organized methods of advertising and marketing, offered this novel barn to attract "progressive" and "wide-awake" farmers.

The tremendous expansion of agricultural prosperity in Iowa and elsewhere during the first two decades of the twentieth century so increased the demand for building plans that older plan services found new competitors entering the field. William Radford, a Chicago architect who put out plans over a twenty-year period, simply beefed up his services. But others, such as William Louden, a barn equipment manufacturer in Fairfield, Iowa, and M. L. King, an agricultural engineer from Iowa State University, now also got into the business. While Radford charged $15 in 1909 to those wanting plans for an octagon barn and $20 for a true-round barn, Louden (who advertised his service as free) offered round barn plans for $5 in 1915.[68] Louden found it advantageous and profitable to supply the plans that would then open a market for his main stock-in-trade: labor-saving equipment.

A case in point is the round barn Louden designed for the farm of Frank Cramlet & Son. The Cramlets, who owned a large cattle and sheep feeding operation three miles north of Douds in Van Buren County, decided in 1921 to build such a barn and turned to the architectural department of the Louden Machinery Company for their plans. A draftsman proceeded to draw up blueprints for what the editor of the Fairfield *Ledger-Journal* lauded to be "as modern a barn as may be found."[69] It featured, of course, "Louden equipment throughout." The basement housed horses and cattle, the second floor contained a harness area and space for five hundred bushels of feed grain along with "some room for the storing of automobiles," while, above, the loft under the large dome roof held up to seventy-five tons of hay.

43-44. The Architecture Department of the William Louden Machinery Company, Fairfield, Iowa, designed this distinctive round barn for Frank Cramlet of Van Buren County, as it did hundreds of other barns for farmers throughout the country. Not missing a trick to sell his barn equipment, as early as 1905 Louden was touting a patented track and hay fork as "the most perfect plan yet devised for handling hay in round barns." The company's catalog, Louden Barn Plans (1915), featured two round barn designs, one of clay tile and the other of wood.

45. When the roof supports for the large dome cupola gave way about 1970 and put the rest of the handsome dome roof structure in danger of collapse, the Cramlets decided to install a less extravagant replacement, namely an asphalt-shingled straight cone roof.

46. The barn as it looks today.

43

44

46

47. This is one of two round barns in Iowa known to have been built according to plans provided by the Permanent Buildings Society of Des Moines, headed by hollow clay-tile advocate Matt L. King. Here we see the barn under construction in 1918 on the Bernard Holtkamp farm in Henry County.

48. The barn as it appears today is in good condition although it is no longer in use.

47

48

49. *Neither pillar nor post supports the roof of this unusual round barn in Franklin County. Instead, as this 1917 view and two others on the next page show, the huge 122-foot diameter roof is held up by galvanized wire cables hooked to rods at the top of the silo.*

The Permanent Buildings Society was another plan service. The head of this Des Moines organization, Matt L. King, had helped originate the "Iowa Type" clay-tile silo and was a leading advocate of using hollow-clay-tile blocks in place of brick for farm buildings. While little is known about his group, one of its activities is clear: it offered advisory service to farmers planning to build. Bernard Holtkamp, who lived near Salem in Henry County, took advantage of the service when building his round clay-tile barn in 1918. After seeing a round wooden barn in adjoining Jefferson County, he visited the office of the society. There he pointed out several features he wanted in a round barn, and they proceeded to prepare a suggested plan. When the secretary of the society mailed Holtkamp the resulting drawing, the secretary noted that it showed "more windows and less doors than we talked of the day you were in the office. This is on account of the absolute necessity of plenty of windows in this type of barn."[70] But, perhaps less concerned than they about light reaching the center of the barn, Holtkamp probably rejected this advice. The resulting barn has numerous doors and relatively few window openings. As was usual, Holtkamp had modified published plans to suit his own needs. The Permanent Buildings Society evidently did not extend its efforts to supervising or constructing such barns, for Holtkamp obtained his materials and labor from the immediate vicinity.

Matt King's most unusual permanent building design was a huge hollow-tile round barn, 122 feet in diameter, built six miles north of Iowa Falls in southern Franklin County. Its size, while noteworthy, could not match the audacity of the barn's flat roof, which was to be totally suspended by wires running down from the top of the silo. Without a single obstructing pillar or post located inside for support, wrote Matt King for the *American Carpenter and Builder* in 1917, the barn amounts to a huge "Umbrella for the Cattle," a gigantic "covered, walled barnyard," in which 300 steers

49

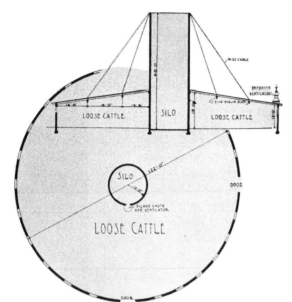

50. At the roof, the cables attach at various points to I-bolts that run through two circles of purlin planks (double 2×10's spiked together) to steel plates beneath.

51. Interior view shows the two lines of purlins to which cables attach for holding up the roof.

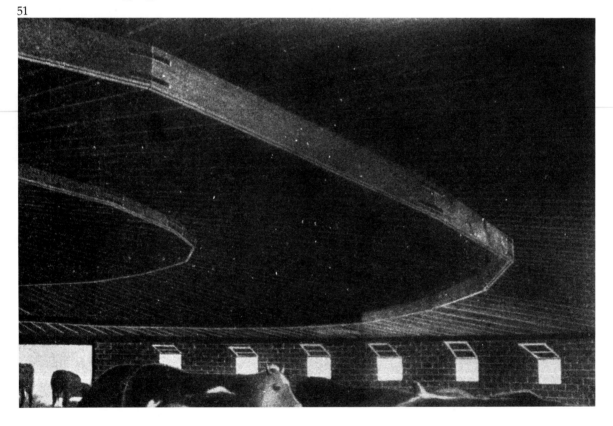

could be sheltered under a twelve-foot ceiling and a hay rack wagon could be turned anywhere "without even going around the silo."[71] Stockman Herman Wood has "gone crazy," ran the story about him in his neighborhood. So often, in fact, did Wood hear the doubts of his friends and neighbors that he began to lose faith in his idea and called in Matt King as a consultant. King, among other things, reassured Wood and proceeded to design the system of cables that stretched down from the top of the silo to each of the two lines of roof purlins below. Although many remained convinced that the silo would never carry the weight, the reckoning of King and Wood ultimately proved correct. Sixty-five years later, the system still continues in operation.

Several round-barn contractors and architects of this era also publicized the results of their labors in builders' and carpenters' magazines. "People come here for miles and miles around" to see his fifty-six foot round dairy barn, boasted builder G. E. Gratke of Strawberry Point. Although visitors first wondered "Is it any good?" he testified that upon inspecting it "they pronounce it all right; for it is convenient and handy."[72] This barn, featured in an illustrated article for *American Carpenter and Builder* (1911), was followed in 1914 by that of another Iowa architect/builder, B. J. Diers. He proudly presented a "rather unusual," immense, ninety-foot diameter round barn that he had erected on the Fry Imperial Stock Farm just south of Granville in Plymouth County. "Few people," Diers stated, "realize the immense amount of floor space contained in a round barn," and the extent of labor saved in feeding when "the silo is located in the center and all the cows are arranged around it."[73] A Charles City man, W. E. Frudden, touted in *Building Age* (1915), the virtues of a round dairy barn of hollow tile erected to the owner's "great satisfaction" on a farm must west of Nashua.[74] Frudden believed that a sixty-foot round barn such as this was "well adapted" to accommodate one row of stalls surrounding a sixteen-foot diameter silo with wide passage-ways both in front and in back of the cattle and a feed alley nearly five feet wide running between the silo and the mangers. "Such an arrangement," Frudden concluded, "results in a great saving of time when feeding the stock."[75] Frudden's enthusiasm for round barns continued in his subsequent book, *Farm Buildings* (1916), in which four of the fourteen barns he featured were true-round barns of clay tile and masonry in Iowa.

52

52. *After building this magnificent 90-foot barn on a Plymouth County farm, B. J. Diers publicized the event among his fellow architect/ builders through the trade publication,* American Carpenter and Builder. *The feature article in 1914 is all that remains of the barn's story, for a tornado destroyed this prominent landmark in 1963.*

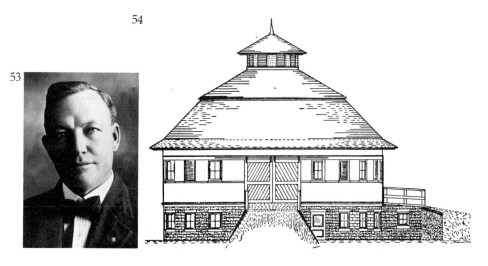

53

54

55

Of the architect/builders who reached beyond trade journals for the broader readership of agricultural newspapers, none seems to have excelled Benton Steele. Between 1907 and 1923 he contributed to numerous midwestern papers, illustrating his latest round barn designs. After working initially to cultivate markets in the Indiana and Wisconsin dairy districts, he shifted his attention farther west to Iowa, Nebraska, and Kansas, moving his office in early 1909 from Pendleton, Indiana, to Halstead, Kansas. By 1910 Steele could boast the success of his most recent plan for a circular barn "built first in northern Indiana and recently duplicated by many farmers in Nebraska and Kansas."[76]

One interested farmer was dairyman Charles Nebergall of Blue Grass Township in Scott County, Iowa. He had somehow learned about one of Steele's barns being built for a man named Hollenbeck near Casey, Iowa, and decided to see it for himself. Having recently lost his own square barn to a tornado and hoping to replace it soon, he took the Rock Island train to Casey, rented a horse and buggy from the livery stable, and headed southwest out of town. When he arrived at the Hollenbeck farm three miles away, what he saw being constructed undoubtedly impressed him. He immediately hired Steele and his traveling crew to build a round barn at his own place, albeit one of different design from the basement-ramp barn at Hollenbeck's. What had led Nebergall to contact Steele in the first place? Perhaps he had read one of Steele's several articles published in *Kimball's Dairy Farmer* of Waterloo, the *Breeder's Gazette* of Chicago, or in *Hoard's Dairyman* of Fort Atkinson, Wisconsin.[77]

Be that as it may, Steele and the Kansas crew lived with the Nebergall family during the spring of 1914 while erecting a handsome fifty-six-foot diameter barn. It combined first-story walls of clay-tile with second-story walls of wood frame sided with vertical board and batten. Steele and his crew kept a busy schedule. "We built four barns after leaving your place," wrote Steele to Nebergall the following January.[78] But now, with a new building season fast approaching, the search for new clients found Steele plying Nebergall with questions: "By the way, have you ever had any more pictures made of the barn?" "How is the building outlook in your neighborhood?" and "Would you give me the name and address of the old gentleman who liked the barn so well?"[79]

53. *Benton Steele (at age 46 in 1912) was actively building round barns and regularly writing to agricultural newspapers with his latest design in hopes of finding customers for his specialty buildings.*

54. *One of Benton Steele's plans that appeared in the Waterloo, Iowa publication,* Kimball's Dairy Farmer.

55. *The prolific round barn builder, Benton Steele, constructed this combined wood and hollow-clay-tile barn near Davenport in 1914 on the Charles Nebergall farm. It is the only example of Steele's handiwork known to still exist in Iowa.*

56

57

58

59

56. *Three times between 1903 and 1910* Wallaces' Farmer *published this plan of a 12-sided stock barn built by Lloyd Z. Jones, an Illinois farmer. Consequently at least three Iowa barns of similar design appeared in Cedar, Ringgold and Warren counties.*

57. *This barn in Washington Township, Ringgold County, resembles the plan of one publicized in* Wallaces' Farmer.

58. *This hollow-clay-tile barn, the prototype for many round barns constructed in Iowa, was built in 1910 by the Johnston Brothers Clay Works near their clay pits located just south of Fort Dodge, Iowa.*

59. *Except for the two sizes of hollow tile used in barns produced by the Johnston Brothers Clay Works, in which a larger clay block begins two courses above the window, clay tile barns all look much the same — smooth walls, a single-story design with loft, and few additions. Variety came in choosing a conical or gambrel roof and in the clay tile itself, which ranged in shades of color from the deep red of the Johnston Brothers tile to a golden tan. Sometimes the tiles varied slightly in hue, which gave a multi-toned effect to the barn.*

Traveling crews like Steele's were not unusual. A farmer having a round barn built in northeastern Tama County brought in a crew from Sioux City to do it. Where this crew gained its experience is a mystery; there are few round clay-tile barns in the northwestern part of the state and none near Sioux City. Perhaps they were masons who traveled the state putting up clay-tile buildings.[80]

Apart from printing articles contributed by enthusiastic builders, midwestern agricultural editors typically covered round barn developments by reporting descriptions and interior layout plans of farmers who had built one. Although the editors and those people who provided plan services and wrote books were not innovators — leaving essentially unmodified the round barn styles devised by experiment stations — they helped supply the farmers' need for more building plans. And, by including at least some round barns, these sources spread the idea of the round barn and the understanding of how to build one.

When clay tile came into use for round barns, several firms — including the Adel Clay Products Company, the Mason City Brick and Tile Company, and the Mt. Pleasant Brick and Tile Company — got into the act. But it was a Fort Dodge clay products manufacturer who quickly assumed leadership in promoting and building them. Only two years after the Ames Experiment Station introduced the first "Iowa type" clay-tile silo, the Johnston Brothers Clay Works, Inc. built probably the first hollow clay tile round barn constructed in Iowa. This was erected in 1910 on the farm adjoining the clay pits as a way of advertising the firm's product. The firm then went on to build at least fifteen more round barns of clay tile in the state. Johnston Brothers barns are easily identifiable by the deep dark color of their tile and the tiles used. Masons used a relatively small size tile to construct the barn's lower portion up to, or a few courses above, the top of the window line. Then they switched to a larger tile for the remaining upper portion. The distribution of Johnston Brothers barns was largely confined to the north central counties.[81]

Publicizing the use of clay tile for round barns in Iowa extended beyond the manufacturer's home office. In at least one area a farmer acted as a salesman for the Johnston Brothers Clay Works, which supplied at a minimum the materials and general plan for the barn. J. G. McQuilkin farmed in northeastern Benton County and sold barns on the side. He built one for himself and then sold at least two others in the neighborhood.[82] McQuilkin's efforts thus yielded three of the company's barns clustered near the dairying area of Black Hawk County. One would be mistaken, however, to assume that the suitability of round barns for northeastern Iowa's growing dairy industry explained his success. The farmers who bought the barns built them for general farming rather than strictly for dairying.

A final impetus to round barn construction came from the Gordon-Van Tine Company of Davenport, which advertised extensively in the *Iowa Homestead, Wallaces' Farmer,* and other midwestern farm papers. Those farmers who shrank from attempting to build in the round could buy the entire barn pre-cut and ready to nail in place. This "makes the purchase of a farm building," in the words of the company, "nearly as simple and devoid of risk as buying a Ford automobile, a Howard watch, a Stetson hat, or a Government bond."[83] To help make its case, Gordon-Van Tine appealed to the authority of agricultural experiment station research, which recommended round barns as enclosing a "greater floor area" than rectangular barns and making easy and "quickly accomplished" the chores of feeding and cleaning. Moreover, the immense hoops comprising the sills, plates, purlin, two cupola rings, and girder were designed, they claimed, with such strength (to handle the considerable outward thrust of the roof on the side walls) that the barn "could be turned on its side and rolled like a hoop without injury to the framework of the barn."[84] Further reassuring the faint-of-heart, the catalog's writers stated:

> Because of lack of familiarity with round barns, carpenters believe them difficult to build. Standard barrel barns are not hard to erect and any good builder, with the help of our plans, can erect one without difficulty. There is really less difficult framing to do in connection with the round barn than in building rectangular barns of truss or braced rafter construction. There are no trusses or braces or wind braces in round barns and no difficult angles to figure. The rafters are the only part of this barn that require any special care in laying out and cutting. We will finish detailed information about how to proceed in building a round barn when requested.[85]

The accompanying plans, they promised clients, "show you exactly where each piece goes — the piece on the plan and the stick of lumber itself are marked exactly the same, so it is simply a matter of following plans and driving nails."[86]

Among the nineteen barn plans featured in the catalog, the company marketed two basic "Barrel Barn" designs: a sixty-foot diameter, fifty-foot high, single-story barn without a silo, and a fifty-four-foot high two-story version built on a three-foot concrete foundation with silo. Each had exterior walls of vertical siding, a self-supporting roof, and a cupola containing sufficient louvers to admit light for the hay loft. For the purchase price, the farmer also got what the company touted as "the only successful hay-loading outfit for round barns that is on the market."[87]

The catalog's single-story Barrel Barn No. 214 especially impressed W. J. Yordy, a Marshall County breeder of Poland China hogs and White Wyandotte chickens, and he ordered one delivered. Yordy had the interior layout modified, however, to resemble that of the catalog's two-story barn plan containing a silo in the center. Shortly thereafter Henry A. Dobbins, who lived four miles away, visited Yordy's new barn and decided it was just what he wanted for his own 320-acre "Elmnole Stock Farm." Dobbins then hired two carpenters from the nearby town of Rhodes to erect, with slight variations, the same mail-order version. And so, by 1919, State Center Township had accommodated another No. 214 Barrel Barn. Both barns stand today in good condition on their respective farms.[88] Yet another barn of the same plan was built in 1919 by a man named Bomgaars for his large sheep-raising operation two miles west of Rock Rapids. Though in deteriorating condition, it still exists and is visible to travelers looking north as they drive along Highway 9.[89]

60-61. Barrel Barn Plan 214 offered by the Gordon-Van Tine company of Davenport, Iowa, in their 1917 catalog. Claiming that their electric-driven machinery system solved the leading problem of barn building — the time-consuming cutting of the dimension or framing lumber — the company catalog pointed out that "we cut all this material to fit at our factories, and ship it, all bundled and marked, so that it reaches you all ready to nail in place."

62. Mr. Bomgaars bought such a pre-cut barn in 1919 for his farm outside Rock Rapids.

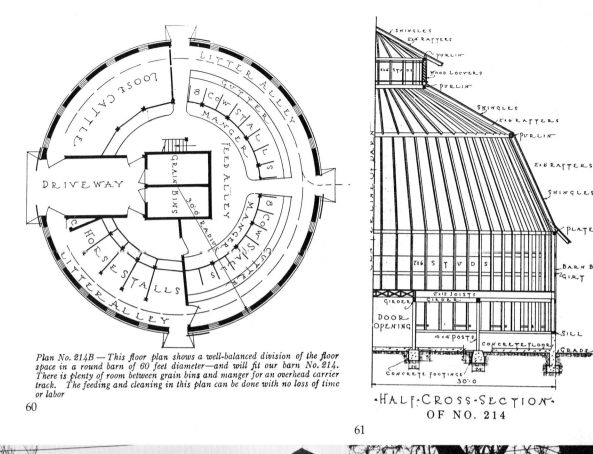

Plan No. 214B — *This floor plan shows a well-balanced division of the floor space in a round barn of 60 feet diameter—and will fit our barn No. 214. There is plenty of room between grain bins and manger for an overhead carrier track. The feeding and cleaning in this plan can be done with no loss of time or labor*

In the floor plan the following labels appear: LITTER ALLEY, LOOSE CATTLE, DRIVEWAY, GRAIN BINS, 30'-0 RADIUS, GUTTER, 8 COW STALLS, MANGER, FEED ALLEY, 8 COW STALLS, MANGER, GUTTER, HORSE STALLS, LITTER ALLEY

HALF·CROSS·SECTION·
OF NO. 214

In the half cross section the following labels appear: SHINGLES, 2x4 RAFTERS, PURLIN, 2x4 STUDS, WOOD LOUVERS, PURLIN, SHINGLES, 2x6 RAFTERS, PURLIN, 2x6 RAFTERS, SHINGLES, PLATE, BARN BOARDS, GIRT, 2x6 STUDS, 2x12 JOISTS, GIRDER, GIRDER, DOOR OPENING, 4x4 POSTS, CONCRETE FLOOR, SILL, GRADE, CONCRETE FOOTINGS, 30'-0

60

61

62

63

The earliest known Gordon-Van Tine barn, built in 1910, is in southwest Davis County. The firm provided Wes and Jess Tarrence with a blueprint and the necessary lumber shipped from Davenport to Moulton. From Moulton, the Tarrences and other farmers in the neighborhood hauled the lumber to the farm by horse and wagon. The resulting barn had the definite appearance of predating the plans of the Illinois experiment station as well as those of the company's later catalog designs noted above. The chief difference lay in its straight conical roof and slender circular cupola, which gave the barn a look derivative of Franklin King's ideas.[90]

Only one other firm — curiously named the Chicago House Wrecking Company — is known to have also sold round barns precut at the factory. William A. Moffitt, who farmed near Mechanicsville, saw a copy of the company's catalog and took a liking to Barn Design No. 106, a fourteen-sided, sixty-foot diameter barn. Soon after he ordered one to be delivered, the materials arrived by rail with the fourteen-foot wide wall sections already assembled. Local carpenters proceeded to erect the barn around an existing silo in about 1914, and thereafter the Moffits used it for their beef cattle operation until its removal about 1957.[91]

Yet, even with the help of promotional schemes by mail-order companies and other individual builders, the idea of circular barns had a hard time catching on. The momentum built up by the enthusiastic claims of round barn proponents began to stall as critics voiced their doubts.

63. *One of near twins that stand in State Center Township of Marshall County.*

Chapter Five:

DOUBTERS CARRY THE DAY

Octagon barn, just east of Iowa City in Lincoln Township, shown in a 1973 pencil drawing by artist Marjorie B. Hayek.

"My ideal dairy barn," wrote one farmer in 1909, "is a round structure... Yet there are plenty of dairymen who would not have a round barn as a gift."[92] This typified farmer attitudes even through the ensuing decade, which became the heyday of round barn popularity and publicity. From the 1880s onward, the barn simply never surmounted resistance to enjoy the kind of undivided support needed for converting most farmers to its use. Enough criticism, faint praise, and outright opposition circulated to keep most farmers cautious and uncertain and to confine the round barn's acceptance to only a few venturesome souls. It took a stalwart disposition to put up a round barn when all one's neighbors were building rectangular barns. The large number of unconvinced farmers prompted writer S. C. Burt to accurately prophesy in 1919: "The round barn is not common...and probably never will be very popular. One may find one or two, perhaps, in a day's drive across country — say in 200 miles."[93]

Agricultural newspaper editors themselves gave little support. They did print correspondence from round barn enthusiasts and from farmers describing barns they had built, but none took it upon himself to promote them as had *Hoard's Dairyman* with the silo. In fact, when they did comment, it was nearly always in the negative.

The editor of *Hoard's Dairyman* objected to "the difficulty of getting sunlight into all parts of the stable; the impracticability of getting a full view of the stable from any point of observation; the necessity for a good many extra steps in feeding grain, milking and hauling out manure," and claimed that the barn's shape did "not readily lend itself to enlargement."[94] I. W. Dickerson of *Wallaces' Farmer* believed that what the farmer saved by needing less material to enclose the same amount of floor and mow space with a circular rather than a rectangular wall would be offset by additional labor costs needed to build this more complicated structure. Also, he thought space gained in the round barn to be "more apparent than real," in that much of it is wasted in the stall arrangement of large round barns. And, if the barn had a silo in the center, the room needed "for the ensilage cutter and the pipe for filling the silo, and for driving in and out with the wagons, means a great deal of space must be left open."[95] The editor of the *Iowa Homestead* expressed his belief that, "no matter how many windows are provided," a round barn approaching 75 feet in width "is bound to be dimly lighted in the interior."[96] Furthermore, he wrote, although a round barn's strength makes it "less liable to suffer in case of bad storms than a rectangular type," the round barn "is difficult to frame for the reason that so many of the angles are other than right angles," which "adds greatly to the work of building and ... increases the cost of the barn considerably."[97] Moreover, the advantage of placing a silo in the center of the round barn to reduce the work of feeding ensilage requires "that the barn must be considerably enlarged, and in doing this the builder is going to needless expense."[98]

Others shared his skepticism. E. L. D. Seymour, writing in his multi-volume work, *Farm Knowledge* (1918), found the barns to be unpopular because, among other things they were difficult to light, hard to arrange satisfactorily, and made it somewhat difficult — given the circular tracks — to install litter carriers and milking machines. Finally, the barn's shape made it difficult to build additions or to combine it with other buildings.[99] The most noteworthy attacks came from C. F. Doane. He was a former student of Franklin H. King, the Wisconsin College of Agriculture professor who originated and advocated adoption of the true-round barn. Although initially accepting King's point of view as a student, Doane's subsequent experience led him to reject it. Upon leaving the university, he had taken up dairy work at the Maryland experiment station, which had "a large barn of the round type" with two silos inside. After a year on the job, Doane concluded that "misconceptions and lack of knowledge," were sustaining the idea of the round barn. The Maryland barn was ultimately torn down, he charged," as not being worth the ground it encumbered for any purpose to which it could be put at that place, and in this conclusion every man who had anything to do with the barn heartily concurred." Not surprisingly, his articles drew spirited rebuttal both from advocates of round barns and from farmers who owned one.[100]

Even Professor King's place of research, the Wisconsin Agricultural Experiment Station, turned its back on the round barn in 1916. Researchers F. M. White and C. I. Griffith found rectangular barns to be more satisfactory than round ones and cited seven reasons why they did. Among them: locating the silo in the center "is inconvenient for filling, and unless care is taken in keeping silage cleaned up the odor from it is objectionable"; some "sacrifice of stable and hay-mow room is made by locating the silo in the barn"; and "it is more difficult to secure proper ventilation in a round than a rectangular barn."[101]

The attacks did not come from farmers who actually put up round barns on their farms. They, in fact, stood as the barn's principal defenders against the critics. In our research we discovered no instances of adverse comment in the agricultural press leveled by first-generation owners. This echoes the view stated by a contemporary observer who, in responding to the charge that "many farmers have built round barns to their sorrow," believed it to be just not so! "In my travels in Wisconsin," he reported, "I have seen many round barns and have yet to find the owner of such a barn who is not perfectly satisfied with it." In fact, "most of them are very enthusiastic on the subject."[102] On the other hand, retorted another, the unwillingness of builders to admit a mistaken investment "might naturally be expected." After all, he stated, "A woman generally speaks well of her husband after she has secured him, however faulty he may be."[103]

While later generations of owners expectedly were more divided in their opinion — farm mechanization having made barns increasingly obsolete — surprisingly few unfavorable comments have come from present owners of round barns. Of thirty-seven who responded to a mail survey question asking them their opinion about the barn's advantages and disadvantages, sixteen stressed its advantages, ten emphasized its disadvantages, and eleven gave mixed reactions. The most commonly cited advantage was ease of feeding animals and the most frequently noted disadvantage was that it contained too much impractical or wasted space.

But the foremost stumbling block to round barn success had nothing to do with the barn's actual usefulness or workability. Rather, writers pro and con agreed, it failed to find acceptance because the vast majority of carpenters and farmers were accustomed to working in time-worn rectangular grooves of habit. The round barn, stated one editor, "is not in keeping with the average farmer's scheme of things; he is in the habit of working on the basis of squares and oblongs and a circular arrangement seems odd and uninviting."[104] Building round structures required knowledge and skill not possessed by the ordinary carpenter; it was very difficult to secure carpenters experienced in round barn construction. These frustrations found expression in one farmer's advice:

> I tried in vain to find an architect or builder who could make working plans or to take a contract to erect a round barn that would meet my needs. So I went to work and made plans of my own and hired workmen by the day....
>
> I would advise anyone who contemplates building a round barn to secure the service of a good builder who has built a round barn before, or one who is familiar with higher mathematics as applied to building. I tried for two years to secure a man of that kind, but failed.
>
> I employed fourteen different mechanics to help me erect my barn and not one could do anything until he was shown, nor could any of them understand any of the principles involved in its construction.[105]

That so many farmers proceeded to build such barns in the face of scant information and the ignorance of architects and builders is testimony to their willingness to experiment and innovate.

By the mid-1920s, however, the tide of opinion had swung away from such round barn experimentation. A report on barn construction, published in 1922 by the Iowa Experiment Station, featured the Tonsfeldt round barn (located outside LeMars). It found the strengths of such barns to be many and their shortcomings few. But by 1925 another circular published by the station entirely reversed the emphasis and concluded abruptly, "while the round barn may meet some requirements, it is not recommended."[106] When in 1927, in almost apologetic fashion, Iowa State College's Fred C. Fenton published his plan for a round barn, the round barn was obviously in decline. Although beginning with the barn's several advantages, the professor of agricultural engineering then felt compelled to list its disadvantages and confess: "As a general rule, the round dairy barn is not a practical proposition." In a thin defense, he believed that "with some persons, and under certain conditions, it does make an appeal and is to be preferred to the rectangular type. For those individuals this plan will be of

64. Rectangular habits of thought died hard, as this abandoned Lyon County octagon barn along Highway 18 near the South Dakota line attests.

65. The last known instance of publicity for the round barn in Iowa occurred in 1927, when Fred C. Fenton's design appeared as "Dairy Farmer Plan No. 9" in The Dairy Farmer, *a Des Moines agricultural journal. For the price of 40 cents, the Dairy Farmer Building Service in Des Moines would send out a set of complete blueprints for constructing the barn.*

65

ELEVATION

especial interest."[107] Whatever remaining enthusiasm farmers had for the round barn, it was doomed soon to end.

Hard times sealed the fate of the round barn. The financially difficult 1920s sharply reduced farmer demands for buildings and dampened further experimental ventures. Publicity for round barns declined as well. The Gordon-Van Tine Company, in their 1926 catalog, printed only their most popular barn plans and eliminated references to round barns shown in earlier catalogs. The Great Depression halted almost all farm construction, and by the time farmers could afford to build again (after the Second World War), round barns — and traditional barns generally — had ceased to be practical.

The round barn fit the time of horse farming. Horses and cattle could stay in stalls near to and around a central feeding area (most often in the teens that meant the enclosed area surrounding the silo). Silage would not freeze in the round barns, and the farmer could toss it down with minimum work in winter. Hay chutes, and sometimes grain chutes, from the loft to the basement floor made the feeding of hay and grain easier. Litter carrier tracks reduced the labor needed to clean out the barn and hay carriers made filling the barn less of a chore. Some barns had ramps leading up to the loft floor, allowing the farmer to drive his wagon straight in and unload. Such conditions were ideal for the round barn and made it admirably suited to this period.

The farm tractor and its impressive accompaniment of large implements changed all that. Even the largest round barn seldom has enough alley space to allow entry of the tractor with its front-end loader, which cuts short the onerous chore of hauling manure. As many an old barn is converted to use as a machine shed, the round barn again proves impractical. It simply cannot house large plows, cultivators, and other modern machinery. So today these barns, along with many of their rectangular cousins, find their use limited to loose housing for pigs and beef cattle or occasional storage space. As often as not, they stand empty, wasting from neglect.

Others rest alone at the edge of, or amid, fields. For those lone survivors of a once-working farmstead, the future is uncertain, as they can expect little future care. But even with the best of care, they are fast passing from the scene — as victims of storm and fire. In just the past five years, for example, we discovered that two had been torn down by their owners, windstorms had claimed three, and two had succumbed to fire.

Additionally, round-barn owners find themselves shouldering an extra burden: paying larger than normal costs whenever the roof needs repair or replacement. Even during the round barn's time of popularity, when advertisers of roofing material featured their product on round barns, writers cautioned those contemplating such a building "to figure on a shingle roof both now 'and forevermore' since this is the only roofing material which can be used without enormous waste."[108] Not surprisingly, present round-barn owners often comment about the expense and difficulty of obtaining non-inflated bids from roofers willing to undertake this unfamiliar job. The extra cost of maintaining such a building for such reduced purposes almost guarantees that many of the few round barns standing today will be only a memory in a few years.

66

67

66. *General-purpose round barns were often converted into hog houses. This one in Jackson County served originally as a sales barn.*

Two casualties to advanced states of disrepair —

67. *a Jasper County octagon barn captured on film before succumbing to the torch about 1978.*

68. *the Lorenzo S. Coffin barn (Webster County) photographed in 1966 shortly before its collapse;*

69. *Broken window panes betray farmers' attitudes when they see little use for the old barn.*

70. *Sprung siding makes clear the ravages of time and inconstant maintenance. It also throws into question the wisdom of using wrap-around horizontal siding. The curving was done by using fairly narrow sawed lumber (rarely clapboard) and nailing the boards securely to the studding. But, as the horizontally-applied siding grew older and stretched and shrank with the seasons, it tended to pull away from the building, exposing the frame to damage from the elements.*

63

69

70

68

At one time in our past the round barn was among the innovative wonders of progressive agricultural change in Iowa. But at one time in our past, so too was the wooden silo, the local creamery, and the steam tractor. The round barn today is old and, by and large, obsolete. But it is still standing on farms across the state — sometimes half fallen down and sometimes dangerous to enter. Why is it still there? For sentimental reasons mainly.

Families take pride in the barn's distinctiveness, in its departure from the typical run-of-the-mill agricultural buildings found on every farm. "At the least," says the editor of the Doon *Press*, a circular barn "was a talking piece and a sort of rural status symbol."[109] Constantly, owners speak with pleasure of the many passersby they have seen stopping to photograph their barn or of artists having painted or sketched it. One owner lovingly features an artist's sketch of his round barn on the masthead of his stationery. Often, round barns are also local landmarks, identifying the area — testimony in itself of their distinctiveness — and local folklore good naturedly circulates many jokes about them, none of which can be printed. They are indeed a rural architectural rarity that makes them something special to those who have them.

71. Alone and vulnerable, this round barn stands at the south edge of suburban residential development in Cedar Falls.

72-73. To attract the customer's eye, building materials firms advertised their wares with sketches of round barns. These items appeared in Wallaces' Farmer *during the years 1905-1906.*

74. Family pride showed in this advertisement placed in the Scott County Atlas *of 1919. That same year, the owner had officially entered his land as Knoll Crest Farm in the state Register of Farm and Homestead Names.*

75. A cheaper alternative to replacing his cedar shingle roof was chosen by this Dubuque County farmer. The result — a less expensive though certainly more unattractive covering of asphalt sheets.

71

72

73

75. *A cheaper alternative to replacing his cedar shingle roof was chosen by this Dubuque County farmer. The result — a less expensive though certainly more unattractive covering of asphalt sheets.*

75

74

76

Rarely has community sentiment come together on behalf of saving this unusual type of building. It happened recently in LeMars, though, where citizens rallied to save the Tonsfeldt round barn from destruction.[110] Peter Tonsfeldt built his barn at the town's edge in 1919 to show purebred livestock and feature the owner's prize polled Hereford bull named Ito's Perfection, believing that the new breed of cattle would revolutionize the livestock industry. But before Tonsfeldt's dream could be realized, financial hard times visited him. Caught in the burden of debt felt by so many in the 1920s — farmers who had bought land at high World War I prices and then struggled under the postwar collapse of agricultural prices — Tonsfeldt's West Urban Stock Farm went under in 1928. Although few today remembered anything about the farm's story, nearly everyone had come to know the large round barn as they entered or left western LeMars on Highway 3. And so when the barn came up on the auction block in 1980 and the farm's purchasers offered it as a gift to the fair board, publicity brought forth an outpouring of public pledges to help pay the necessary costs of moving and repairs. Finally, on a September morning in 1981, the round barn began its trek through LeMars to a new home (see photo). By the next morning its movers had reached their destination — the fairground at the town's east side, where a new foundation had been built at one end of a recreated pioneer village.

Barns such as these ought to be of more than simply family or local interest. We need to better appreciate their features, to more fully understand their place in time, and take steps to help preserve the few that remain. Round barns inform us of an era when questions of how to improve farm practices in Iowa moved many to try more efficient means of bringing hay, grain, pasturage, and animals together under one roof. The round barn represented an important part of that effort.

Much of the charm attached to round barns is, of course, intangible. Their shape, being unexpected on Iowa farms, is striking — curving walls and uninterrupted roof lines impart a clean, pure form, and the great interior loft gives dramatic effect. To walk through one is to journey into a past of bygone tasks and different needs, when this silent partner on the farm stood as the Iowa farmer's principal building. The round barn is a representation of that time and is something belonging to those years. Today, when a round barn is explored, such a time, for a moment, is captured. One can only hope that future generations will also have their chance to explore them.

78. Sunlight fills the cupola above and filters down through the cracks and roof spaces to the loft below.

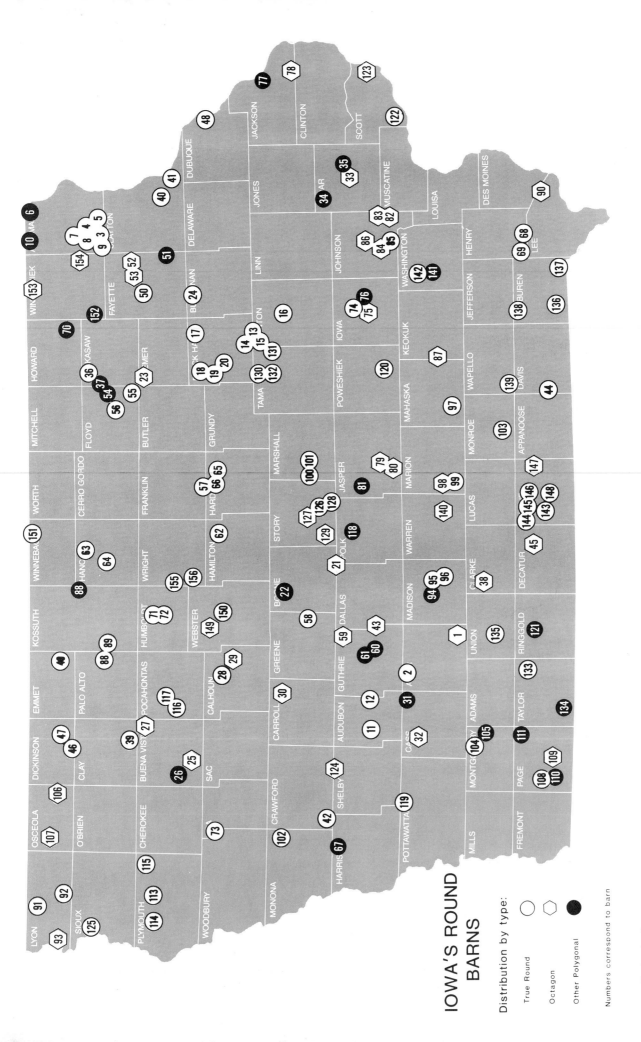

IOWA'S ROUND
BARNS

Distribution by type:

◯ True Round

⬡ Octagon

⬤ Other Polygonal

Numbers correspond to barn

Scale of miles

0   10   20   30

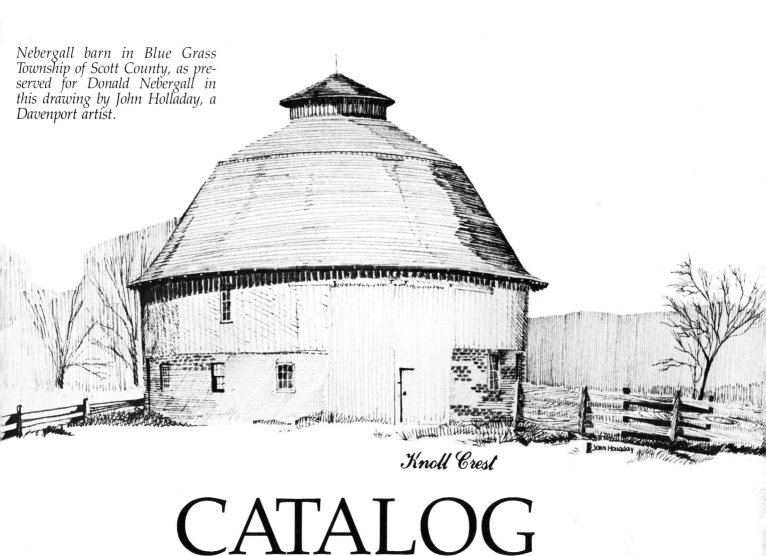

Nebergall barn in Blue Grass Township of Scott County, as preserved for Donald Nebergall in this drawing by John Holladay, a Davenport artist.

Knoll Crest

CATALOG OF ROUND BARNS

What follows is an entry, including a photograph whenever possible, for every true-round, octagon, or other polygonal barn we could find. Following this catalog is a list of selected barn characteristics along with the identity of all barns (noted as barn entry numbers) that possess that characteristic. The catalog does not include barns for which information proved either too sketchy as to their existence and location or too vague concerning their features. Additionally, only round barns that existed on farms are included here. The number assigned to each entry corresponds to that found on the map of sites printed nearby. The catalog entries are arranged alphabetically by county and township, and numerically by section within each township.

1. ADAIR COUNTY, Union Township, Section 16

Octagon Hog Barn, year built unknown
Owner when built: Unknown
Architect/Builder: Unknown

This eight-sided barn, no longer in use, has balloon frame construction with horizontal drop siding. A large central cupola with octagonal cone roof rests upon an eight-section wood-shingled roof supported from within. Additional light is admitted into the interior through a window inserted in each section of the roof.

Photo: Lowell J. Soike, 1982

2. ADAIR COUNTY, Walnut Township, Section 7

True-Round Barn, 1912 (roof collapsed in 1969, remainder razed 1978)
Owner when built: Hollenbeck
Architect/Builder: Benton Steele, Halstad, Kansas

Of ramp barn design, 60 feet in diameter, with a basement and a second-story level reached by a driveway ramp, under which a milk house with water tank and a small room (perhaps for calves) existed. An interior hollow-clay-tile silo measured 15 feet in diameter. A concrete and brick foundation supported hollow-clay-tile walls tied together with reinforcing rod. The roof was of a dome type with wood shingles. The basement interior was arranged with daisy stanchions and a feed rack encircling the silo; the second level contained hog and chicken areas, a tool room, a grain bin, and hay storage space.

Photo: Donald B. Powell, 1969

3. ALLAMAKEE COUNTY, Franklin Township, Section 19

True-Round Barn, 1914
Owner when built: A. W. Swenson
Architect/Builder: Otto Sanders, carpenter

The wood frame is of native logs sawed into dimension plank lumber erected on a foundation 10 feet high and 2 feet thick, made with stone quarried on the farm. Pine vertical siding covers the exterior walls. Sheltering

all is a self-supporting gambrel roof with gable-roofed hay dormer and metal aerator. Inside the 50-foot diameter barn is open interior space with a hay manger running around the exterior wall. The manger is fed by means of hay chutes located at points along the outside perimeter of the loft story above. In order to convert the loft space from loose hay to heavier baled hay storage, the owner has since reinforced the floor with steel beams and posts. It is described in Wilson L. Wells, Barns in the U.S.A. (San Diego, California: Acme Printing Co., 1976).

Photo: Frank Hunter, 1979

4. ALLAMAKEE COUNTY, Franklin Township, Section 19

True-Round Barn, year built unkown
Owner when built: Unknown
Architect/Builder: Unknown

The barn has an older center portion with a newer lean-to wing extending three-fourths around it. The central section has a two-pitch gambrel roof with metal aerator on top, a large gable-roofed hay dormer on the north side, and a small dormer on the east. The walls have board and batten siding.

Photo: Lowell J. Soike, 1982

5. ALLAMAKEE COUNTY, Franklin Township, Section 29

True-Round Barn, 1911
Owner when built: Elba Lamborn
Architect/Builder: Unknown

Framed with home-sawed oak 2"x4" resting on a concrete foundation, the Lamborn barn

has a ground level dairy cattle area, a loft level above, and a central hay chute in the middle. Its exterior walls are covered with vertical siding. The roof is of a two-pitch gambrel type with gable-roofed hay dormer and original metal aerator. In 1959 asphalt shingles were applied over the original roof of cedar shingles, and the owner added a milk house to the east side in 1962. The interior dairy cattle area has a circular arrangement with feed manger, cow stanchions, and gutter surrounding a central hay chute. Additional information found in Wilson L. Wells, Barns in the U.S.A. (San Diego, California: Acme Printing Co., 1976).

Photo: Lloyd V. Lamborn, 1979.

6. ALLAMAKEE COUNTY, Iowa Township, Section 10

Twelve-Sided Barn, 1914
Owner when built: Thomas Reburn
Architect/Builder: Unknown

This unusual beef cattle barn is 46 feet diameter with a 14-foot diameter silo that extends up through, and one story beyond, the barn roof. The roof of the silo, originally the same pitch as that of the barn, blew off in a storm during the mid-1950s and was replaced. Concrete block construction characterizes the barn foundation and silo. The interior is arranged in circular fashion with a feed alley surrounding the silo at which fifty cattle can simultaneously eat. Reburn's barn, located just southwest of New Albin, is featured in Wilson L. Wells, Barns in the U.S.A., (San Diego, California: Acme Printing Co, 1976).

Photo: Frank Hunter, 1979

7. ALLAMAKEE COUNTY, Ludlow Township, Section 12

True-Round Barn, 1912
Owner when built: Meyer
Architect/Builder: Unknown

This 56-foot diameter model is of bank barn design, with a lower story of stone and a second, wood framed loft, reached by a ramp embankment built onto its north side. This is only one of the few wood barns in Iowa with horizontal sawn wood siding. The two-pitch

73

gambrel roof is self-supporting with asphalt shingles and still has its original metal aerator. Of special interest is the barn's interior central silo — either of a King or Gurler type — which is constructed of wood stave and lined with cement inside. Such silos were popular until the 1910s but are exceedingly rare today.

Photo: Frank Hunter, 1979

8. ALLAMAKEE COUNTY, Post Township, Section 2

True-Round Barn, year built unknown
Owner when built: Unknown
Architect/Builder: Unknown

Little is known about this one. The barn features an interesting combination of horizontal sawn wood siding for the first floor and board and batten for the second. Its weathered gray siding shows advancing years and abandonment in its pieces of loose siding, missing batten, broken windows, and hanging doors. Surprisingly, the wood shingled, two-pitch, self-supporting gambrel roof is in reasonably good shape, as is the gable-roofed hay dormer and the metal aerator topped by a horse weather vane. The barn's diameter is an estimated 40 feet. Inside is a central feeding hay chute in the middle with dairy cattle stanchions around it.

Photo: Tamara Tieman, 1979

9. ALLAMAKEE COUNTY, Post Township, Section 33

True-Round Barn, 1905 (removed 1982)
Owner when built: John A. Hart
Architect/Builder: Raymond Schules

When originally built around an existing silo, this 53-foot diameter barn had a straight cone-shaped roof supported midway by a row of posts about 6 feet from the silo. This was replaced between 1936 and 1938, when owner Henry Althouse hired contractor John Powell to erect a two-pitch gambrel roof with gable-roofed hay dormers. The barn was framed of home-sawed oak, elm, and basswood studs. The foundation was of clay block covered by bricks resting on concrete footings. Upper-story walls were covered with horizontally applied 1"x8" drop siding. There was a milk house on the south side. The

round barn is featured in Wilson L. Wells, Barns In the U.S.A. (San Diego, California: Acme Printing Company, 1976). It was located about ¼ mile north of Postville on Highway 51.

Photo: Lowell J. Soike, 1979

10. ALLAMAKEE COUNTY, Union Township, Section 17

Twelve-Sided Barn, year built unknown
Owner when built: Unknown
Architect/Builder: Unknown

A basement-type barn with a ramp to the loft, it has a self-supporting, two-pitch gambrel roof with metal roofing. On top of the twelve-section roof is a cupola with an octagonal cone-type metal roof.

Photo: Lowell J. Soike, 1982

11. AUDUBON COUNTY, LeRoy Township, Section 30

True-Round Barn, year built unknown
Owner when built: McCleren
Architect/Builder: Unknown

The barn has board and batten siding, a two-pitch, wood-shingled, gambrel roof with conical-roofed wood cupola. There is no silo in the center, but the interior is arranged in a circular fashion.

Photo: Lowell J. Soike, 1982

12. AUDUBON COUNTY, Melville Township, Section 36

True-Round Barn, 1916
Owner when built: Thomas Campbell
Architect/Builder: Pres. Faultz, carpenter; Bert, stone mason

A general purpose clay-tile barn 60 feet in diameter and 18 feet high to the eaves. The hollow-clay-tile block, since painted white, came from Adel, Iowa. The roof, of two-pitch gambrel design with a hay dormer and gable roof overhang, was replaced after a windstorm took it off in 1959.

Photo: Frank Hunter, 1979

13. BENTON COUNTY, Bruce Township, Section 3

True-Round Barn, 1910
Owner when built: Unknown
Architect/Builder: Probably Johnston Bros. Clay Works, Ft. Dodge, Iowa

This is one of sixteen hollow-clay-tile round barns believed built by Johnston Bros. Clay Works and one of the three throught to have been sold locally for the firm by James Greer McQuilkin. The barn has the small red clay tile in the lower story and larger tile above that characterized the Johnston Bros. design. It is 60 feet in diameter with a 12-foot diameter clay-tile silo inside and has a straight conical roof with asphalt shingles. Use of the barn throughout its existence has been confined to cattle feeding, using an open interior arrangement with temporary dividers. The farm also has a round garage/machine shed built of clay tile.

Photo: Frank Hunter, 1979

14. BENTON COUNTY, Bruce Township, Section 5

True-Round Barn, 1914
Owner when built: Unknown
Architect/Builder: Probably Johnston Bros. Clay Works, Ft. Dodge, Iowa

One of sixteen hollow-clay-tile round barns believed built by Johnston Bros. Clay Works and one of three thought to have been sold locally for the firm by James Greer McQuilkin. The small red tile in the lower story and the larger tile above characterized the Johnston Bros. design. It has a diameter of 50 feet with a clay-tile silo in the center that measures 12 feet across. The straight conical roof is wood shingled and has its original metal aerator atop the dome of the silo. Inside is a circular arrangement, in which four double horse stalls face the central silo on one side, and on the other there is open space where milking stanchions once stood.

Photo: Frank Hunter, 1979

15. BENTON COUNTY, Bruce Township, Section 18

True-Round Barn, 1918

Owner when built: James Greer McQuilkin

Architect/Builder: Probably Johnston Bros. Clay Works, Ft. Dodge, Iowa

One of sixteen hollow-clay-tile round barns believed built by Johnston Bros. clay works. The small red clay tile in the lower story and the larger tile above characterized the Johnston Bros. design. The barn, 60 feet in diameter with a 14-foot diameter silo in the center, has a cone-shaped roof with gable hay dormer and asphalt shingles. One-fourth of the ground floor interior space was devoted to horse stalls before their removal. The area is now open loose housing — one-half for hogs the other half for cattle. Featured in Wilson L. Wells, Barns in the U.S.A. (San Diego, California: Acme Printing Co., 1976).

Photo: Frank Hunter, 1979

16. BENTON COUNTY, Jackson Township, Section 36

True-Round Barn, year built unknown.

Owner when built: Unknown

Architect/Builder: Unknown

A hollow-clay-tile, basement-type barn with the second story entry reached via a ramp from the hillside part of the building. Diameter of the barn is an estimated 60 feet. A three-pitch gambrel roof extends up to near the top of a central clay-tile silo. Comprising the interior space is a cement feed bunk surrounding a 16-foot diameter silo, The round barn is not presently in use.

Photo: Frank Hunter, 1979

17. BLACK HAWK COUNTY, Lester Township, Section 20

True-Round Barn, year built unknown

Owner when built: Unknown

Architect/Builder: unknown

This hollow-clay-tile barn, located just north of Dunkerton, is a highly visible landmark in the area. The white stone lintels supporting the load over the door and window openings stand out in contrast to the darker clay tile walls. A two-pitch gambrel roof with metal aerator has, in its lower part, a large gable roof hay dormer on the north side, along with two small, flat roof dormers on the southeast and southwest sides, and there are windows in the upper pitch of the roof to admit light into the loft.

Photo: Lowell J. Soike, 1982

18. BLACK HAWK COUNTY, Washington Township, Section 23

True-Round Barn, 1915-1916

Owner when built: Unknown

Architect/Builders: Unknown

This barn achieved some popularity through W.E.Frudden's stories written for the February 3, 1917 issue of Country Gentleman and for his book, Farm Buildings (1916). Both stories contain a photo, a ground-floor plan and a cross section drawing of the barn. It measures 60 feet in diameter with hollow-clay-tile walls and a self-supporting gambrel roof with cedar shingles. The central clay-tile silo has, in its upper portion, a clay-tile water tank of a kind devised at the Ames experiment station. A circular arrangement is found inside, with twenty-nine dairy cow stanchions facing inward toward the silo. The concrete barn floors and cow stalls have the added feature that wood blocks treated with a preservative covered the floors in the stall area.

Photo: Lowell J. Soike, 1979.

19. BLACK HAWK COUNTY, 5102 South Main Street, Cedar Falls

True-Round Barn, year built unknown.

Owner when built: Unknown

Architect/Builder: Unknown

No information could be found about this barn, located on the outskirts of Cedar Falls. It was built of hollow clay tile with a two-pitch gambrel roof, and windows located near the eaves as well as on the ground floor help ensure that enough light reaches the center of the barn.

Photo: Lowell J. Soike, 1979

20. BLACK HAWK COUNTY, About 5000 South Main Street, Cedar Falls

True-Round Barn, year built unknown

Owner when built: Unknown

Architect/Builder: Unknown

Little is known about the history of this wood-frame bank barn. Erwin Mohling reports in Wilson L. Wells Barns in the U.S.A. (1976) that "the first story contains twenty-seven steel cow stanchions halfway around the barn" while "the balance of area has horse double stalls and grain bins." A poured concrete foundation wall extends up to the circle of basement-level windows above which wood frame and vertical siding take over. The diameter of the barn is an estimated 83 feet. The enclosed drive to the second floor is formed by concrete retaining walls filled with earth.

Photo: Lowell J. Soike, 1979

21. BOONE COUNTY, Douglas Township, Section 36

Octagon Barn, ca. 1875 (year demolished unknown)

Owner when built: J.F. Hopkins

Architect/Builder: Unknown

A small barn by comparison with the rectangular barns at the farmstead, it perhaps served as a carriage house. The eight-sided building was portrayed in The Andreas Atlas (1875).

Photo: From an engraving in A.T. Andreas' Illustrated Historical Atlas of the State of Iowa (1875, reprinted, Iowa City: Iowa State Historical Society, 1970), p. 317.

22. BOONE COUNTY, Pilot Mound Township, Section 9

Six-Sided Barn/Machine Shed, year built unknown

Owner when built: Unknown

Architect/Builder: Unknown

The history of this building is unknown. The exterior walls are of board and batten siding with two windows in each of its six sides. A set of double doors open to the southwest. The roof forms a self-supporting hexagonal cone with a window inserted at the midpoint of its three southern-most sections. Asphalt shingles were applied over the wood shingles sometime in the late 1970s.

Photo: Frank Hunter, 1979.

23. BREMER COUNTY, Polk Township, Section 7

Octagon Barn, 1887
Owner when built: Unknown
Architect/Builder: Unknown

The date "1887" is in wooden numerals above the main double doors. The eight-sided barn has a wood shingled, octagonal, cone-shaped roof on top of which may once have rested either a cupola or a windmill. Horizontal shiplap siding covers the exterior walls, which contain few window openings. The front half of the barn's interior space is open, with livestock pens taking up the rear portion. Hay is taken up to the mow floor above through a large opening inside the front entrance.

Photo: Frank Hunter, 1979

24. BUCHANAN COUNTY, Hazelton Township, Section 17

True-Round Barn, year built unknown.
Owner when built: Unknown
Architect/Builder: Probably Johnston Bros. Clay Works, Ft. Dodge, Iowa

One of sixteen hollow-clay-tile round barns believed built by Johnston Bros. Clay Works. The small red clay tile in the lower story and the larger tile above characterized the Johnston Bros. design. This is the only working barn that we found being operated as it was when built. That is, a Mennonite family — still using horses — keeps the round barn well maintained and in full original use as a dairy enterprise. The estimated 70-foot diameter barn has a two-pitch self-supporting gambrel roof with gable hay dormer and cupola. The interior has a central clay-tile silo around which are cow stanchions facing the feed alley.

Photo: Frank Hunter, 1979

25. BUENA VISTA COUNTY, Hayes Township, Section 17

Octagon Barn, 1907-1908 (burned down about 1918)
Owner when built: Joseph A. Haines & Sons, Lake View Farm
Architect/Builder: Unknown

Only the cement foundation remains of this 72-foot diameter horse barn. A floor layout plan and engraving of the barn were featured in an April 30, 1908 issue of the Iowa Homestead. Vertical siding covered the barn's balloon frame, which was composed of cottonwood lumber sawed on the farm. A straight cone-type roof held a gable roof hay dormer and wood cupola. As for the interior arrangement, a 12-foot driveway passed through the center from north to south. A row of nine horse stalls ran along the west side, and behind them, along the outer wall, there were two box stalls, with a harness room in between. Another box stall was located on the west side just inside the north entrance. On the half east of the driveway, there was a box stall at the north entrance followed by a row of six horse stalls running east and west. The remaining southeast portion of the barn had a large carriage room with feed bin. Behind all the horse stalls ran a litter carrier on a track, and the loft above was fitted with a circular track for the hay fork.

Photo: Engraving of north and west facades in Des Moines *Iowa Homestead*, April 30, 1908.

26. BUENA VISTA COUNTY, Nokomis Township, Section 17

Six-Sided Barn/Machine Shed, 1927
Owner when built: G.F. Ericksen
Architect/Builder: G.F. Ericksen and Charles Sansen

The 40-foot diameter building ably fit the time when there was a need to store a large volume of small horse-drawn equipment, but its suitability has declined, as the size of the doors proved unable to accommodate much of the newer large equipment. The frame of the building is of dimension plank lumber resting on a concrete foundation. Horizontal drop siding covers the exterior walls. The six-section cone roof is self-supporting and has wood shingles. Exterior doors are located on the north, south, and east sides.

Photo: Frank Hunter, 1979

27. BUENA VISTA COUNTY, Poland Township, Section 15

Octagon Barn, before 1908 (year demolished unknown)
Owner when built: W.H. and C.D. Ruebel
Architect/Builder: Unknown

Built as a heated sales pavilion for regular public auctions of their poland china hogs and shorthorn cattle, little else is known about the barn except for this farm photo, which appeared with announcements of forthcoming sales in Wallaces' Farmer.

Photo: From *Wallaces' Farmer* 33 (Nov. 13, 1908), 1392.

28. CALHOUN COUNTY, Sherman Township, Section 30

True-Round Barn, unknown construction date
Owner when built: Unknown
Architect/Builder: Unknown

One of four in Iowa known to have had a dome roof, it has asphalt shingles over wood. Vertical board and batten siding covers exterior walls that rest upon a cement foundation. Inside is a central silo. The ground floor had horse stalls in one half and stanchions in the other half. This farm also had a round central-drive corn crib with a similar dome roof, but this has reportedly been recently torn down.

Photo: Frank Hunter, 1979

29. CALHOUN COUNTY, Sherman Township, Section 32

Octagon Barn, year built and demolished unknown
Owner when built: Unknown
Architect/Builder: Unknown

Information about this one come from two sources. Eugene Newhouse of the Calhoun County Historical Society wrote to Kent Sissel in 1968 of "an octagon barn west of Twin Lakes on a farm that was owned by the Featherstone family," which had been torn down. Then, in 1979, Judy Webb of the Calhoun County Historical Society spoke to Milton Heins, an owner of a round barn in Section 30, Sherman Township, who reported that adjacent to him, in Section 32, there had once been "an octagon barn with a silo in the center...."

No photo available

30. CARROLL COUNTY, Jasper Township, Section 32

Octagon Barn, 1883
Owner when built: Unknown
Architect/Builder: Unknown

The modified hip-roof form and non-circular interior arrangement appears derivative of Lorenzo Coffin's octagon barn (1867) in Webster County. Its time of construction followed on the heels of publicity for Coffin's barn that appeared in the Iowa Home-stead. The barn is 66 feet in diameter, and its walls are of board and batten siding resting on a stone foundation. The roof has asphalt shingles and a square cupola with the year 1883 on it. A rectangular interior arrangement has cattle enclosure space located in the basement. Above, a central driveway runs through the middle with hay and machinery storage on one side and two granaries, with horse stalls between, on the other. The barn is discussed in Richard Westerfield, "There's Character in Barns," Iowan 12 (Spring 1964), 36-40

Photo: Frank Hunter, 1979

31. CASS COUNTY, Grant Township, Section 20

Sixteen-Sided Barn, ca. 1915
Owner when built: Unknown
Architect/Builder: Bert Willison, builder and former farm resident

A one-story barn with a conical roof comprising sixteen pie-shaped sections, the exterior walls have vertical sawed wood siding. The interior space originally contained a central wood-stave silo around which was a continuous feed trough for feeding silage to livestock. But after 1930 the barn's owner removed the silo, substituting eight posts to support the roof, and converted the building to a machine shed. Presently, however, the barn's use has returned to that of a livestock shelter. Each of the sixteen sides of the barn measures 10 feet. Each side has a window, and there is a set of double doors on both the north and south sides. The barn is described in Centennial History Book of Anita: A Century Unfolds, 1875-1975, p. 321.

Photo: From *Centennial History Book of Anita*

32. CASS COUNTY, Grove Township, Section 8

Octagon Barn, year built unknown
Owner when built: Unknown
Architect/Builder: Unknown

Located on 22nd Street across from the golf course at the south edge of Atlantic, the eight-sided barn appears structurally sound, although the exterior walls and roof have fallen into disrepair. Erected on a concrete foundation, board and batten siding covers the walls, which support an octagonal cone-shaped, wood-shingled roof that has, on its east side, a large gable-roof hay dormer.

Photo: Lowell J. Soike, 1982

33. CEDAR COUNTY, Center Township, Section 4

Octagon Barn, ca. 1875 (year removed unknown)
Owner when built: William L. McCroskey, Waveland Farm
Architect/Builder: Unknown

By the look of this engraving, the octagon barn built here served merely as a small auxiliary building to that of the adjacent substantial rectangular barn. The present owner of the farm reports that the octagon barn no longer existed by the time they bought the place, which was forty years ago.

Photo: From an engraving in *A.T. Andreas Illustrated Atlas of the State of Iowa*, (1875, reprinted, Iowa City: Iowa State Historical Society, 1970), p. 338.

34. CEDAR COUNTY, Pioneer Township, Section 23

Fourteen-Sided Barn, ca. 1914 (torn down about 1957)
Owner when built: Moffit
Architect/Builder: Chicago House Wrecking Company, Design No. 206

Delivered pre-cut by rail from the Chicago House Wrecking Company with the flat sections already constructed, Moffit hired local carpenters to erect it for his beef cattle operation. The barn was 60 feet in diameter

with a 16-foot diameter wood stave silo in the middle. It had horizontal drop siding placed over balloon frame studding and a two-pitch self-supporting gambrel roof with asphalt shingles. The barn's design departed from the published plan in two major respects: it had three large drive-through doors with none of the small individual doors shown in the plan, and the distance between the main roof and that of the cupola was wider in order to have alternating windows and ventilators inserted in the wall of the cupola. The circular interior arrangement duplicated that of the plan in having a feed alley between the silo and a row of stanchions that encircled it.

Photo: From a photocopy of the catalog plan.

35. CEDAR COUNTY, Springfield Township, Section 20

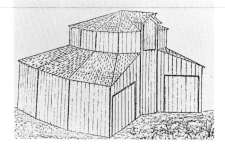

Twelve-Sided Barn, built early 1900s (torn down early 1940s)
Owner when built: Fred J. Hartwig
Architect/Builder: Echoes plan for Lloyd Z. Jones stock barn in Illinois.

The shape of this barn, with its tall central section and surrounding wing shed, is similar to that of a nine-sided barn in Ringgold County and an 8-sided model in Warren County. The plan resembles one published on the stock barn of Illinois farmer Lloyd Z. Jones in Wallaces' Farmer 28 (Jan. 16, 1903), 74, and reprinted in issues of October 25, 1907, and June 17, 1910. The center part measured 20 feet across and the wing shed 12 feet. Poles held up the center section of the barn. The barn was used for feeding loose hay to beef cattle. For more details, see the (July 1980) issue of the Cedar County Historical Review, 64.

Photo: From a drawing in the *Cedar County Historical Review*, (July, 1980), 64.

36. CHICKASAW COUNTY, Deerfield Township, Section 4

True-Round Barn, 1916
Owner when built: George Darrow
Architect/Builder: Unknown

A diamond pattern of dark tile worked into the lighter colored hollow-clay tile above the main double doors distinguishes this barn. Diameter of the barn is an estimated 64 feet

and that of the clay tile interior silo, 14 feet. The self supporting roof is of a two-pitch gambrel type and has its original wood shingles, along with windows for lighting the loft, inserted near the roof's midpoint. The circular arrangement inside has dairy stanchions in one half, and the other half is devoted to horse stalls facing the central silo. Further details are in Wilson L. Wells, Barns in the U.S.A. (San Diego, California: Acme Printing Co., 1976).

Photo: Lowell J. Soike, 1979

37. CHICKASAW COUNTY, Deerfield Township, Section 6

Twelve-Sided Barn, 1912
Owner when built: Donald and Ray Duncan
Architect/Builder: Al Bartlett, contractor

This is of a design also used in constructing the Nicholson ten-sided barn located 2½ miles away in Floyd County, which has the same features: successive alternating window and door openings, two windows above the main door entrance, a small window built into the roof, vertical sawed wood siding, and an unusual two-pitch gambrel roof constructed of pie-shaped sections. Its original cupola has inscribed on it the year 1912. Each side of the barn is 14 feet wide. Framing lumber is of 2"x6" home-sawed cottonwood 2"x6" timbers. A wood silo, 14 feet in diameter and 35 feet in high, is inside. Several panels of 2-foot-wide sections of horizontally applied boards comprise the silo's walls.

Photo: Frank Hunter, 1979

38. CLARKE COUNTY, Madison Township, Section 32

Octagon Barn, 1870, according to present owner (burned down in 1977)
Owner when built: Unknown
Architect/Builder: Andrews Bros.

The barn measured about 55 feet across. Built on a stone foundation, the walls had vertical wood siding. The shape of the non-self-supporting roof was something unto itself: two of its eight sections were built as a gable in which the ridge was level with the peak of the roof. The interior frame was built of heavy timbers with mortise and tenon connections.

Photo: Raymond Johnston, 1967.

39. CLAY COUNTY, Herdland Township, Section 17

True-Round Barn, year built unknown.
Owner when built: Unknown
Architect/Builder: Probably Johnston Bros. Clay Works, Ft. Dodge, Iowa

One of sixteen hollow-clay-tile round barns believed built by Johnston Bros. Clay Works. The small dark-red clay tile in the lower story and the larger tile above characterized the firm's design, as did the frequently used conical metal roof. A large hay dormer with gable roof eased the storage of hay. In the center of the barn there is a hollow-clay-tile silo with a metal dome roof that is probably a replacement for an original conical type.

Photo: Frank Hunter, 1979.

40. CLAYTON COUNTY, Jefferson Township, Section 16

True-Round Barn, year built is unknown
Owner when built: Unknown
Architect/Builder: unknown

Located in a beautiful setting, the visual qualities of the basement-type round barn are enhanced by its distinctive gambrel roof, which combines round and sectional cone elements. The wood frame walls, covered with vertical board and batten siding, are erected on a stone foundation. It is not known whether a silo exists inside.

Photo: Frank Hunter, 1979

41. CLAYTON COUNTY, Millville Township, Section 10
True-Round Barn, 1915-1916
Owner when built: Unknown
Architect/Builder: Xavier Jacque, carpenter

Two details of particular interest are the metal siding covering the exterior walls, and the dome-shaped roof, which is one of four known in the state. The extent to which the roof is self-supporting is problematical, because it has an unusually strong system of timber frame reinforcement that appears — in its use of rather long timber members extending from the perimeter of the loft floor to the roof's midpoint — to be an elaboration of the Shawver roof truss. Entry to the loft floor of this bank barn is by a ramp constructed of earth between concrete retaining walls. A 12-foot diameter wood stave silo is inside. Half of the lower level is devoted to stanchions for dairy cattle facing inward around the silo. The other half has loose housing pens and a milk room. In the loft above, a driveway passes to the side of the silo, near which is a granary and feed room space, with the remaining area for hay storage. Originally a general purpose barn, it is now used for hogs and beef cattle.

Photo: Frank Hunter, 1979

42. CRAWFORD COUNTY, Boyer Township, Section 34

True-Round Barn, year built unknown
Owner when built: Unknown
Architect/Builder: Unknown

This is the smallest known round-clay-tile barn in Iowa. It has a straight conical roof with a metal aerator on top. Unfortunately, the roof has deteriorated, which has exposed the loft to rot. Mortar is also missing from between the tiles.

Photo: Lowell J. Soike, 1982

43. DALLAS COUNTY, South Main Street, Linden

Octagon Barn, year built unknown

Owner when built: Unknown
Architect/Builder: Unknown

This eight-sided barn, in sad disrepair and with a partially collapsed roof, is of interest because the exterior walls are clad with corrugated metal sheeting, which is unusual. Diameter of the barn is an estimated 60 feet. It has a two-pitch gambrel roof comprised of trapezoidal sections. In the center of the barn there is a hollow-clay-tile silo of 18-foot diameter, around which there are five horse stalls on one side and fifteen cattle stanchions on the other. Outside, a low shed extends along two sides.

Photo: Frank Hunter, 1979

44. DAVIS COUNTY, West Grove Township, Section 7

True-Round Barn, 1911
Owner when built: John and Rose Wallace
Architect Builder: Gordon-Van Tine Co., blueprint design, Davenport, Iowa; carpenters were Bill Anderson, Jess Tarrence and Wess Tarrance.

This is the earliest known example of a round barn evidently designed by architects of the Gordon-Van Tine Company, a provider of pre-cut barns. The plan departs from later catalog versions in having a straight conical, rather than gambrel, roof.

Photo: Lowell J. Soike, 1979.

45. DECATUR COUNTY, Center Township, Section 9

Ten-Sided Barn, 1905
Owner when built: Aaron Goodman
Architect/Builder: Aaron Goodman

Located along Highway 69 between Leon and Van Wert, this ten-sided barn has a ten-section conical roof, with asphalt shingles, extending up to a large cupola with a similar roof. Around the cupola, window openings alternate with wood louver vents. The exterior walls are of board and batten. The barn, built by owner Aaron Goodman, accommodated 12 head of horses, a corncrib and haymow. A pulley system was used to draw hay up into the haymow from a wagon pulled into the central driveway. Goodman's neighbor, Ed Schultz, liked the barn so much that

he built a duplicate version on his farm, but it later burned down.

Photo: Lowell J. Soike, 1982

46. DICKINSON COUNTY, Millford Township, Section 29

True-Round Barn, year built unknown
Owner when built: Unknown
Architect/Builder: Unknown

The history of this barn is not known. It has dark-brown clay-tile walls erected on a concrete foundation and a two-pitch gambrel roof with an attached silo. The building is presently used for raising hogs.

Photo: Lowell Soike, 1982.

47. DICKINSON COUNTY, Millford Township, Section 31

True-Round Clay-Tile Barn, year built unknown
Owner when built: Unknown
Architect/Builder: Unknown

This is a large dark-brown clay-tile barn resting on a concrete foundation with a two-pitch gambrel roof. Neither its history nor interior arrangement is known.

Photo: Lowell Soike, 1982

48. DUBUQUE COUNTY, 2810 N. Cascade Road, Dubuque

True-Round Barn, 1915
Owner when built: Unknown
Architect/Builder: Probably Johnston Bros. Clay Works, Ft. Dodge, Iowa

One of sixteen hollow-clay-tile round barns believed built by Johnston Bros. Clay Works. The smaller red clay tile in the lower story and the larger tile above characterized the company's design. A large gabled granary in the loft projects out from the roof, as does a smaller gabled dormer to the side. The conical roof, which has had roll roofing put over its wood shingles, is supported from within by timbers extending from the loft's perimeter to a purlin rib below the roof's midpoint. Diameter of the barn is 60 feet, with a 14-foot diameter hollow-clay-tile silo located inside. The interior was originally used for dairying, with cow stanchions and horse stalls arranged in a circle facing the silo. The stanchions have since been converted to a fence and cement feed bunk. Above, the loft has some grain storage room, but most of the space is for hay.

Photo: Frank Hunter, 1979.

49. EMMET COUNTY, Armstrong Grove Township, Section 34

True-Round Barn, 1911-1912
Owner when built: Unknown
Architect/Builder: Unknown

A low-pitched gambrel roof and a first floor of cement block distinguish this barn's appearance. It has a diameter of 65 feet, and of particular interest, a central wood stave silo 16 feet in diameter remains in place though not in use. Surrounding the silo on the ground floor are cow stalls on one side, horse stalls on the other, and two pens in the rear. There is a circular hay track in the hay loft above. The barn was taken out of use in 1969.

Photo: Frank Hunter, 1979

50. FAYETTE COUNTY, Center Township, Section 15

True-Round Barn, year built unknown
Owner when built: Unknown
Architect/Builder: Probably Johnston Bros. Clay Works, Ft. Dodge, Iowa

One of sixteen hollow-clay-tile barns believed built by Johnston Bros. Clay Works. The

79

smaller red clay tile in the lower story and the larger size above characterized the firm's design, as did the frequent use of a straight conical roof with gable hay dormer. Interior arrangement of its space is unknown. The building has not been in use for several years.

Photo: Tamara Tieman, 1979.

51. FAYETTE COUNTY, Fairfield Township, Section 26

Twelve-Sided Barn, 1906 (clay tile silo likely replaced earlier one of wood)
Owner when built: August Nus
Architect/Builder: Unknown

This distinctive barn is one of three of this type known to have been built in Iowa. The diameter of the barn is 60 feet and that of the silo, 14 feet. Asphalt shingles protect the old wood shingled roof and horizontal wood siding covers the exterior wood frame walls. The interior is open, with a feed bunk situated around the central silo.

Photo: Lowell Soike, 1979

52. FAYETTE COUNTY, Pleasant Valley Township, Section 23

Octagon Barn, ca. 1880s (removed mid-1960s)
Owner when built: Unknown
Architect/Builder: Joe Butler, West Union, Iowa, carpenter

Although this one is gone, another just like it built shortly thereafter still exists three miles away on section 23 of Union Township. Built on a stone foundation with horizontal drop siding over a heavy timber frame, the barn walls supported an octagonal cone roof with a gable-roof hay dormer. The interior of the barn was split down the center with a central driveway and arranged in rectangular fashion, with cattle and horses housed in straight rows. The barn is discussed in Richard Westerfield, "There's Character in Barns," Iowan 12 (Spring 1964), 48

Photo: Joan Liffring-Zug, 1964

53. FAYETTE COUNTY, Union Township, Section 23

Octagon Barn, late 1880s
Owner when built: Grimes
Architect/Builder: Joe Butler, West Union, Iowa, carpenter

The octagonal, cone-shaped, self-supporting roof of this barn is in the tradition of the 1880s octagons promoted nationally in the writings of Elliott W. Stewart. But the construction of a gable hay dormer and the use of horizontal shiplap siding mark it as something unto itself. The barn is modeled on another that Butler built three miles east of here, which has since been torn down. The heavy-timber-framed wall sections of white pine rest on a stone foundation. The interior space has a central driveway with stalls on either side along its length. According to the son of the first owner, the barn was converted in later years from general beef cattle and horse sheltering purposes into a modern dairy barn with steel equipment, water bowls, and cork brick floors. Other additions included a milk house and clay tile silo.

Photo: Joan Liffring-Zug, 1964

54. FLOYD COUNTY, Niles Township, Section 14

10-Sided Barn, 1915
Owner when built: John Nicholson
Architect/Builder: Henry Krumroy, carpenter

This barn has essentially the same design as the Duncan twelve-sided barn 2 1/2 miles away in Chickasaw County. This is visible in the succession of alternating window and door openings, two windows above the main door entrance, a small window built into the roof, vertical sawed wood siding, and in the unusual two-pitch gambrel roof constructed of pie-shaped sections. The roof has wood shingles and a metal aerator. A central silo originally located inside the 54-foot diameter barn has since been removed.

Photo: Frank Hunter, 1979.

55. FLOYD COUNTY, Riverton Township, Section 23

True-Round Barn, ca. 1914
Owner when built: A.R. Brooks
Architect/Builder: Unknown

Publicity came to this barn in two contemporary stories written by W.E. Frudden, one in the June 1915 issue of Building Age and the other in his book, Farm Buildings (1916). Both stories contain a photo, descriptive information, and plans showing the interior arrangement. The two-pitch gambrel roofed barn has a diameter of 60 feet and a clay tile silo measuring 16 feet across in the center. Twenty-one windows provide plenty of sunlight to the circular interior arrangement. The basement plan shows half of its space for dairy cattle stanchions made of pipe embedded in concrete and the other half divided into calf pens. The main-floor plan shows a horse barn in which nine double horse stalls concentrically surround over half of the area around the silo. A driveway runs along one side of the silo for a wagon to enter and exit via two sets of double sliding doors, while the space remaining on the other side of the drive contains three grain bins.

Photo: Frank Hunter, 1979.

56. FLOYD COUNTY, St. Charles Township, Section 10

True-Round Barn, 1914
Owner when built: John Spotts
Architect/Builder: Johnston Bros. Clay Works, Ft. Dodge, Iowa

One of sixteen hollow-clay-tile round barns believed built by Johnston Bros. Clay Works. The smaller red clay tile in the lower story and the larger tile above characterized the firm's design. The barn is about 55 feet in diameter with a silo in the center that measures 12 feet across. The two-pitch gambrel roof and gable-roofed hay dormer have had wood shingles replaced with ones of asphalt. A close look at the window frame reveals that its design was patented by Johnston Bros. Clay Works in 1912.

Photo: Dennis Marsh, 1979

57. FRANKLIN COUNTY, Grant Township, Section 31

True-Round Barn, 1916
Owner when built: Unknown
Architect/Builder: Unknown

This is one of four such distinctive barns known in Iowa and the only one constructed of clay tile. It also differs from the others in having a flat, rolled-asphalt roof that is not held up by posts from below but suspended by cables from the silo. Inside is a 20-foot diameter clay tile silo that housed feed until its use was discontinued about 1974. The interior space is divided into pie-shaped pens which the owners use for gestating sows. The first owner of the barn reportedly used it for raising sheep, and then for many years an owner put it to use for feeding cattle. As for the barn's advantages and disadvantages, Its owners say that the barn has the advantage of providing a lot of space, but that the roof upkeep is costly.

Photo: Frank Hunter, 1979.

58. GREENE COUNTY, Junction Township, Section 35

True-Round Barn, 1911
Owner when built: Henry A. and Martha Frantz
Architect/Builder: Beecher Lamb

This is the only round barn in Iowa known to have its design based directly on plans contained in the Illinois experiment station bulletin. The major departure is in its having masonry (concrete block), instead of wood frame, construction. Oral tradition has it that the bad winter of 1909 made the owner long for the convenience of one building for everything. So within two years he had a builder constructing this 55-foot diameter beef cattle barn with two-pitch gambrel roof and wood cupola and a silo in the center measuring 16 feet across and 60 feet tall. Two sets of double exit and entrance doors on the upper level of this bank barn were reached by concrete ramp driveways. The owner converted the barn from beef to dairy purposes in the 1930s, and for the next forty years its owners milked and fed a herd of about three dozen cows. More details about the barn's history are contained in Wilson L. Wells, Barns in the U.S.A. *(San Diego, California: Acme Printing Co., 1976) and W.E.*

Frudden Farm Buildings (Charles City, Ia.: The Author, 1916), p.15.

Photo: Frank Hunter, 1979

59. GUTHRIE COUNTY, Richland Township, Section 15

Octagon Barn, ca. 1881
Owner when built: Unknown
Architect/Builder: Unknown

This eight-sided barn, with its modified hip-roof form and rectangular interior arrangement, appears to have derived from the plan of Lorenzo Coffin's octagon barn (1867) in Webster County. It is approximately 70 feet in diameter — 28 feet per side — and mainly differs from Coffin's barn in being built in a bank-barn style with an inclined drive to the loft floor instead of being built into a hillside with basement and upper-level entries. Wood shingles cover the roof, the top of which once supported a cupola. Shuttered upper-level windows and horizontal wood siding visually distinguish the exterior walls.

Photo: Frank Hunter, 1979.

60. GUTHRIE COUNTY, Valley Township, Section 3

Twelve-Sided Hog Barn, year built unknown
Owner when built: Unknown
Architect/Builder: Unknown

This dilapidated one-story building, with its disproportionately high roof, lies abandoned at the west edge of the farmstead. Horizontally applied wood boards are used as siding for the barn's balloon frame construction while, above, wood shingles cover both the twelve sections of its main roof and those of the large conical-roof cupola.

Photo: Lowell J. Soike, 1982

61. GUTHRIE COUNTY, Victory Township, Section 34

Six-sided barn, year built unknown (torn down about 1970)
Owner when built: Unknown
Architect/Builder: Unknown

This six-sided barn measured an estimated 30 feet across and was being used for hogs up to the time of its discontinuance. Horizontal

drop siding covered its frame of dimension plank lumber. The conical roof was constructed of 6 pie-shaped sections with a cupola on top.

Photo not available.

62. HAMILTON COUNTY, Blairsburg Township, Section 26

True-Round Barn, ca. 1910
Owner when built: William T. Oakland
Architect/Builder: Unknown

The clay tile barn originated as a combination hog and sale barn with hog farrowing below and a sales ring on the upper level. The diameter of the round barn is 50 feet; inside is a central clay-tile silo of 16-foot diameter. The interior space is presently open on both levels. The upper sales area is well lighted owing to the row of windows located just below the break in the two-pitch gambrel roof. The self-supporting roof has asphalt shingles, a small dormer in the rear and a metal aerator. Entrance to the loft floor is through double doors via an earth-filled ramp with concrete retaining walls, and there is also a gable-roofed dormer entry.

Photo: Frank Hunter, 1979

63. HANCOCK COUNTY, Crystal Township, Section 24

True-Round Barn, pre-1915
Owner when built: Unknown
Architect/Builder: Probably Johnston Bros. Clay Works, Ft. Dodge, Iowa

One of sixteen hollow-clay-tile barns believed built by Johnston Bros. Clay Works. The smaller dark red clay tile in the lower story and the larger tile above characterized the firm's design, as did the frequent use of a straight conical metal roof with gabled hay dormer. The silo no longer has its roof, and what remains of the barn roof is in poor condition.

Photo: Lowell J. Soike, 1982.

64. HANCOCK COUNTY, Erin Township, Section 7

True-Round Barn, ca. 1916 (tornado damaged; removed 1981)
Owner when built: Link Gray
Architect/Builder: Probably Johnston Bros. Clay Works, Ft. Dodge, Iowa

The hollow clay tile barn is one of sixteen believed built or sold by Johnston Bros. Clay Works. The smaller dark red clay tile in the lower story and the larger tile above characterized the firm's design. It measured 72 feet across and in the center there was a 20 x 55-foot clay tile silo. The two-pitch wood shingled gambrel roof had a metal aerator on top. About 1980 a tornado collapsed the roof, and the remainder was torn down the following year. A photo and description of the barn is contained in Recollections of Britt, Iowa, 1878-1978, p. 90.

Photo: Frank Hunter, 1979

65. HARDIN COUNTY, East Hardin Township, Section 22

True-Round Barn, year built unknown
Owner when built: Unknown
Architect/Builder: Probably Johnston Bros. Clay Works, Ft. Dodge, Iowa

One of sixteen hollow-clay-tile round barns believed built by Johnston Bros. Clay Works. The smaller dark red clay tile in the lower story and the larger tile above characterized the firm's design. Nothing is known about the barn's interior arrangement, past uses, or other aspects of its history or specifications.

Photo: Frank Hunter, 1979

66. HARDIN COUNTY, Hardin Township, Section 14

True-Round Barn, 1915
Owner when built: Unknown
Architect/Builder: Probably Johnston Bros. Clay Works, Ft. Dodge, Iowa

One of sixteen hollow-clay-tile barns believed built by Johnston Bros. Clay Works. The smaller dark red clay tile in the lower story and the larger tile above characterized the firm's design. The barn has a central silo within and a two-pitch gambrel wood-shingle roof with attractive gabled hay dormer above. The roof sports two metal aerators, one on either side of the silo.

Photo: Frank Hunter, 1979

67. HARRISON COUNTY, Allen Township, Section 14

Twelve-Sided Barn, 1912
Owner when built: William B. Haner
Architect/Builder: Comstock Construction, Omaha, Nebraska, contractor

William Haner, a carpenter with Comstock Construction, decided — for reasons of barn strength and novelty — to build this barn on his hilltop farmstead. After laying a foundation of unusual two-foot long cement blocks and securing part of the lumber salvaged from the old Olympus Church, he erected a 54-foot diameter barn of twelve sides, 14 feet per side. The two-pitch gambrel roof constructed of pie-shaped sections originally had a metal roof, but this was replaced by wood shingles in 1951. A gable-roofed hay dormer is attached on the south side. Originally used as a cattle barn to shelter purebred Herefords and horses, its present use is for grain, hogs, and cattle.

Photo: Frank Hunter, 1979.

68. HENRY COUNTY, Jackson Township, Section 32

True-Round Barn, 1918
Owner when built: Bernard J. Holtkamp
Architect/Builder: Permanent Buildings Society, Des Moines — plans

This is one of the two hollow-clay-tile barns evidently built according to plans prepared by the Permanent Buildings Society, the head of which was M.L. King, a leading advocate of the use of clay tile in farm buildings. The 50-foot diameter barn has a two-pitch gambrel roof with metal aerator and windows set in to light the loft interior. The circular arrangement of space inside the lower level finds horse stalls and pens installed around a central hay chute area. The upper level, reached by an earth ramp, houses hay, grain, and machinery. The attractive clay tile came from the Mt. Pleasant Brick and Tile Manufacturing Company.

Photo: Frank Hunter, 1979

69. HENRY COUNTY, Salem Township, Section 22

True-Round Barn, 1920s
Owner when built: Unknown
Architect/Builder: Unknown

This round barn's appearance makes its close ancestry to the circular silo clear. It is made of vertical cement staves held in place by metal bands. The farmer built it as an open-space sales arena in the 1920s, but it has since been converted to housing machinery. Diameter of the barn is 36 feet. The straight conical roof has asphalt shingles and a metal aerator.

Photo: Frank Hunter, 1979

70. HOWARD COUNTY, New Oregon Township, Section 15

Sixteen-Sided Barn, ca. 1920
Owner when built: Horky and Andra
Architect/Builder: Unknown

Built originally to show English shorthorn cattle, a later owner adapted it to dairy cattle in 1958 and readapted it again in 1968 for pigs and feeder cattle. The barn, with a diameter of 70 feet and a central cement silo measuring 13 feet across, rests on a stone foundation. Vertical sawed wood siding sheaths its heavy timber frame. A self-supporting two-pitch gambrel roof of sixteen sections is covered with metal roofing. The lower level has pie-shaped stalls that face inward toward the silo, while the loft floor above is open.

Photo: Frank Hunter, 1979

71. HUMBOLDT COUNTY, Delana Township, Section 36

True-Round Barn, ca. 1916 (torn down, 1977)
Owner when built: T.G. and A.B. White
Architect/Builder: Benton Steele, Halstead, Kansas

This was reportedly one of four such barns built for the White Brothers on each of the farms they owned; another was near Emmetsburg. It measured 60 feet in diameter and had a two-pitch gambrel self-supporting roof with wood shingles and conical roof cupola. Uncharacteristically, the barn had no clay tile silo inside. Instead, in the middle, four 12 x 12-inch posts supported a 6,500-bushel-capacity oat bin located in the loft and, in semi-circular fashion around the posts, there was a manger for dairy cows on one side and one for horses on the other. A photo with brief description appeared in the January 15, 1923 and December 1, 1925 issues of a farm journal, The Dairy Farmer, published in Waterloo.

Photo: 1916 view, loaned by Oral Strachan, an owner of the former barn.

72. HUMBOLDT COUNTY, Grove Township, Section 19

True-Round Barn, year built unknown (destroyed by windstorm, 1980)
Owner when built: Unknown
Architect/Builder: Unknown

A one-story barn with loft above, the building rested on a foundation of stone. It had vertical wood siding on the exterior walls and a two-pitch gambrel roof with wood shingles and cupola.

Photo not available.

73. IDA COUNTY, Douglas Township, Section 29

True-Round Barn, early 1900's
Owner when built: Unknown
Architect/Builder: Unknown

This unusual barn features a large, round central section — three stories in height — to which is attached a main-entrance section with gable roof hay dormer that projects outward to a point flush with the exterior walls of a wing shed surrounding the central section. Vertical wood siding clads the exterior walls.

Photo: Lowell J. Soike, 1982

74. IOWA COUNTY, Hilton Township, Section 19

True-Round Barn, 1912
Owner when built: Gustave H. Plagmann
Architect/Builder: Unknown

This huge hollow-clay-tile barn measures an estimated 100 feet across and is the largest such barn in Iowa. It is of a basement barn type with two main entries below and one above. The two-pitch gambrel self-supporting roof is crowned with a metal aerator. Inside is a 16-foot diameter silo around which are hay bunks in the basement level. The second story, at ground level, has horse stalls surrounding the silo. Behind each stall is a trap door to throw manure down to the basement level. In the loft space above, there are seven chutes through which hay is passed to the floor below.

Photo: Lowell J. Soike, 1982

75. IOWA COUNTY, Hilton Township, Section 31

Octagon Barn, year built unknown
Owner when built: Unknown
Architect/Builder: Unknown

The history of this building is unknown. Above the walls of horizontal wood siding, an eight section roof extends up to a large circular silo or cupola that is topped by a cone roof with a small gable dormer. It is being used for beef cattle at present.

Photo: Lowell J. Soike, 1982

76. IOWA COUNTY, Hilton Township, Section 33

Twelve-Sided Barn, 1902 (torn down about 1949)
Owner when built: B.H. Hakes & Son
Architect/Builder: Unknown

Within a few months after completing the barn, owner B.H. Hakes provided for the May 23, 1903 issue of Wallaces' Farmer a description of the building, along with a photo and floor plan. The barn was erected after completing the 20-foot diameter wood stave central silo in 1901. The foundation for the estimated 75-foot diameter barn was constructed of stone. Vertical wood board siding covered the frame, which consisted of standard dimension lumber with the heaviest timbers being 4 x 4's. The single-story barn (8-feet to the eaves) had a sectional cone roof, supported from within by posts containing at least two small gable-roofed dormers (located two-thirds of the way up to the central cupola). On the north side there was a large gable hay dormer, "14-feet high and wide enough for the loft hay track to be level with the top of the silo." Hakes arranged the interior in a circular fashion with two rows of cattle stalls facing a 6-foot manger that ran between the silo and the outside wall. Above the manger a steel track suspended a car that could carry up to ten bushels of feed from the silo to any part of the manger. Another track for a manure carrier ran around the outside of the stalls.

Photo: From a photo in Wallaces' Farmer 28 (May 29, 1903), 798.

77. JACKSON COUNTY, Bellevue Township, Section 29

Six-Sided Barn, 1921
Owner when built: Dyas
Architect/Builder: Stuart, carpenter

Of the four single-story-flat roof barns in Iowa with a silo projecting through the center, this is the only six-sided barn among them. It is a general purpose building, 50 feet in diameter, with horizontal sawed wood siding over the dimension plank lumber frame. Metal covers the roof of both barn and silo, although the latter is probably of more recent origin. The interior is arranged in a circular fashion with pie-shaped stalls placed around a central wood stave silo.

Photo: Frank Hunter, 1979

78. JACKSON COUNTY, Van Buren Township, Section 27

Octagon Barn, 1920
Owner when built: Unknown
Architect/Builder: Gus Klenney

Originally built as a sales barn, the open interior space is now used for hogs. The 50-foot diameter barn has walls framed of dimension plank lumber with vertical sawed board siding. A conical roof comprised of pie-shaped sections — each with a window — extends up to a metal aerator at the apex.

Photo: Frank Hunter, 1979

79. JASPER COUNTY, Fairview Township, Section 11

Octagon Barn, 1904 (burned down, about 1978)

Owner when built: Unknown

Architect/Builder: Unknown

Originally used as a dairy barn and later for general farm use, the eight-sided building had horizontal drop siding and an octagonal roof with asphalt shingles and cupola.

Photo: Karen Gilbertson, Central Iowa Regional Association of Local Governments (CIRALG) Architectural Survey, 1978

80. JASPER COUNTY, Fairview Township, Section 23

Octagon Barn, year built unknown

Owner when built: Unknown

Architect/Builder: Unknown

This is one of two almost identical octagon barns in the township, but little is known about the history of either. The barn, which rests on a concrete foundation, has shiplap horizontal siding applied over a frame that combines dimension plank lumber and heavy timber with interlocking joints. The 54-foot diameter building has an eight-section roof with a large gable hay dormer that extends from roof peak to the eave. At one time a windmill or cupola may have crowned the roof. A gable-roof rectangular shed in back attaches to two sides of the octagon barn.

Photo: Frank Hunter, 1979

81. JASPER COUNTY, Poweshiek Township, Section 28

Twelve-Sided Barn, 1911

Owner when built: Averland

Architect/Builder: Unknown, plans reportedly came from Ames

In its exterior appearance, this barn resembles the design of the Duncan barn (Chickasaw Co.) and Nicholson barn (Floyd Co.). Similarities include a two-pitch gambrel roof formed from twelve pie-shaped sections; windows above the main door, with alternating door and window openings in each wall section; and the absence of a basement level. The main differences are that its sawed wood siding is horizontally rather than vertically applied and that it lacks loft windows inserted in the roof. Diameter of the barn is 60 feet. Inside, the space is arranged in stalls around what was once a central silo. The silo has since been removed and a pole inserted in the middle to support the floor above.

Photo: Frank Hunter, 1979

82. JOHNSON COUNTY, Lincoln Township, Section 2

Octagon Barn, mid-1880s

Owner when built: Unknown

Architect/Builder: George Frank Longerbeam, Downey, Iowa

Located near the Secrest octagon barn, this substantially smaller barn is closely related to it, having the same unusual type of curved laminated-beam roof construction. The single-story barn with loft is arranged inside with a central driveway and stalls on either side. A rectangular shed with tin roof is attached on the south side of the barn. The eight-sided building is in disrepair and sits alongside a circular metal grain bin in the middle of a field.

Photo: Lowell J. Soike, 1982

83. JOHNSON COUNTY, Scott Township, Section 25

Octagon Barn, 1883

Owner when built: Joshua Hunt Secrest

Architect/Builder: George Frank Longerbeam, Downey, Iowa

A beautiful eight-sided basement-type barn just west of Downey, this barn's 80-foot diameter gives it a presence exceeded only by the striking appearance of its graceful bell-shaped roof. The barn's structural sophistication—in its innovative laminated-beam roof—makes the building an outstanding example of rural architecture that, in 1974, qualified it for entry in the National Register of Historic Places. A miniature octagon cupola with similar roof form rests on top of the barn. In the early 1900s, the owner attached a long rectangular feed shed with gable roof on the north side of the barn and then in turn added a tile and cement silo to the feed shed's north end. The basement level of the barn was built for livestock, the ground level for machinery, and the upper loft for loose hay storage. Featured in Wilson L. Wells, Barns in the U.S.A. (San Diego, California: Acme Printing Co., 1976).

Photo: Frank Hunter, 1979

84. JOHNSON COUNTY, Sharon Township, Section 2

Octagon Barn, 1883

Owner when built: John E. Roberts

Architect/Builder: Schrock, carpenter

The plan for this bank-type barn appears to be derivative of Lorenzo Coffin's octagon barn (1867) in Webster County, which was the subject of a long article in a January 1883 issue of the Des Moines Iowa Homestead. The two barns shared the unususal modified hip-roof form and the non-circular interior arrangement. The lower story contained two rows of cow stanchions in the center, horse stalls on one side, a cattle shed on the other, and pens at either end. The ground level had a driveway in the center, with hay, machinery, and grain bin storage space to the side. Featured in Wilson L. Wells, Barns in the U.S.A. (San Diego, California: Acme Printing Co., 1976).

Photo: Lowell J. Soike, 1979

85. JOHNSON COUNTY, Sharon Township, Section 14

True-Round Barn, 1918-1920

Owner when built: Joseph Miller

Architect/Builder: John Schrader, carpenter

Built on a slope, this basement-type round barn has its lower level devoted to cow stanchions facing inward toward feed bunks that surround a clay tile silo. The drive-in loft space is used for hay and grain storage with a large oat bin on one side and a hay fork riding a circular track above. Diameter of the barn is 60 feet and that of the central silo is 10 feet. The two-pitch gambrel roof has wood shingles and a metal aerator. Additional details about the barn are found in Wilson L. Wells, Barns in the U.S.A. *(San Diego, California: Acme Printing Co., 1976).*

Photo: Frank Hunter, 1976

86. JOHNSON COUNTY, West Lucas Township, Section 21

Octagon Barn, year built unknown
Owner when built: Unknown
Architect/Builder: Unknown

The history of this barn is unknown. It is a single story structure with loft, the exterior walls of which have horizontally applied sawed wood siding. The sectional cone roof has a large projecting gable-roof hay dormer.

Photo: Frank Hunter, 1979

87. KEOKUK COUNTY, Warren Township, Section 20

Octagon Barn, late 1870s (razed, 1965)
Owner when built: George Davenport
Architect/Builder: Unknown

Our main source of information is a news article prepared at the barn's demise and based on conversations with the farm's present owner, Quincy Rice. The article, written by Mrs. James Souer, is "Landmark near Delta, an eight-sided barn, no longer

stands," Oskaloosa Daily Herald, *Nov. 27, 1965. The barn was built according to the specifications of George Davenport, which were based on a similar barn he had seen when he visited relatives in Greene County. The timbers were of white pine hauled from Washington, Iowa, and erected over a rock foundation. Built on a ramp-barn plan with basement, ground floor, and loft, the barn had heavy-timber framing with wooden pegs and square nails, vertical tongue-and-groove white pine siding, and a cupola that was later lost to a 1948 windstorm. The barn was 45 feet high from ground level to the base of the cupola. Its modified hip-roof design indicates that the barn plan probably derived from Lorenzo Coffin's octagon barn, which had been built in 1867 in adjoining Webster County.*

Photo: Keith Bryant, 1965, courtesy of Oskaloosa *Daily Herald.*

88. KOSSUTH COUNTY, Buffalo Township, Section 2

Eleven-Sided Barn, 1910-1912
Owner when built: Unknown
Architect/Builder: Ben Longbottom

This attractive barn, with its two-pitch gable projecting hay dormer and unusual conical-roofed cupola, is 46 feet in diameter. Vertical sawed boards cover a dimension plank lumber frame. The two-pitch gambrel roof, built of eleven pie-shaped sections, is covered with wood shingles. Inside, the space is arranged around a 14-foot diameter wood stave silo.

Photo: Frank Hunter, 1979

89. KOSSUTH COUNTY, Whittemore Township, Section 7

True-Round Barn, 1914 (destroyed by fire, 1981)
Owner when built: William F. Dau
Architect/Builder: Owner designed and built, with assistance of Emil Braatz

A July 1916 issue of Wallaces' Farmer reprinted a lengthy item from the editor of the Kossuth Advance about this barn. The article termed it "one of the neatest and best built barns we were ever in." The barn's most novel feature was its exterior walls, which

are all sided with 8-inch shiplap and then covered with galvanized metal siding. It was 50 feet in diameter with a 10-foot diameter wood stave silo in the center. The 6 × 6 inch sill and 4 × 6 inch plate, as with other true-round barns, were built up on 1-inch boards soaked, curved, and nailed together to a perfect circle. Iron cow stanchions encircled the silo on one side, with horse stalls and feed, and milk rooms on the other. A litter carrier on a track added to the convenience of the barn. It had just been converted to lambing operations (including painting and new doors) when it was completely destroyed by fire.

Photo: Frank Hunter, 1979

90. LEE COUNTY, Denmark Township, Section 34

Octagon Barn, 1912
Owner when built: Asa Houston
Architect/Builder: Asa Houston designed and built it

The framing of this 60-foot diameter barn is novel in that dimension plank lumber is used for the walls and roof rafters, while an interior frame of posts and beams built of heavy timbers and held together by wooden pegs supports the eight-section gambrel roof. A driveway runs through the center of the barn. On one side are cow stanchions in a semi-circle facing a grain bin. On the other side is a straight row of horse stalls behind which is box stall space. Asphalt shingles protect the roof.

Photo: Frank Hunter, 1979

91. LYON COUNTY, Allison Township, Section 35

True-Round Barn, 1919
Owner when built: Mr. Bomgaars
Architect/Builder: Gordon-Van Tine Co. "Barrel Barn No. 214" design, Davenport, Iowa

Bomgaars' cylinder barn has all the earmarks of the "Barrel Barn" plan portrayed in Gordon-Van Tine Farm Buildings *(1917), a catalog of mail-order pre-cut buildings available from the Davenport manufacturer. This is one of three known barns of this design in Iowa. The diameter of the barn is about 66 feet. Its balloon frame construction has vertical sawed wood siding and a two-pitch gambrel roof with asphalt shingles. Originally used for dairy and horse shelter with a circular arrangement of interior space, it has since been taken out of service except for storage purposes.*

Photo: Lowell J. Soike, 1982

92. LYON COUNTY, Garfield Township, Section 15

True-Round Barn, 1904
Owner when built: Charles B. Reynolds
Architect/Builder: Owner design based on ideas of F.H. King and Joseph Wing

This barn achieved publicity as "an Iowa Round Barn" in an article by Joseph Wing in an August 16, 1905 issue of the Chicago Breeder's Gazette, and in editions of the Gazette's Farm Buildings book, which reproduced plans drawn from the journal. The main difference between the original photos and the barn as it now exists is in the roof. It originally had a straight conical design with a large windowed cupola. This has since been replaced by a wood shingled, two-pitch, self-supporting gambrel roof with a smaller, but nonetheless attractive, louver-vented cupola. The exterior walls have horizontal drop siding. The interior space is divided rectangularly along lines recommended to Reynolds by Joseph Wing.

Photo: Lowell J. Soike, 1982

93. LYON COUNTY, Lyon Township, Section 16

Octagon Barn, year built unknown
Owner when built: Unknown
Architect/Builder: Unknown

This eight-section conical-roofed barn has two features of visual interest: an oblong and a rectangular addition on each of the barn's two opposing sides, and horizontal woodsiding on one half of the octagon barn with vertical sawed wood on the other. The history of this barn and its changes over time are unknown. It is no longer in use.

Photo: Frank Hunter, 1979

94. MADISON COUNTY, Lincoln Township, Section I

Twelve-Sided Barn, year Built unknown
Owner when built: Unknown
Architect/Builder: Unknown

An unusual single-story barn constructed of concrete exterior walls with steel joists and wood framing inside to support the roof. A large pyramidal cone cupola rises above a twelve-section conical roof.

Photo: Iowa State University architectural windshield surveyor, 1976

95. MADISON COUNTY, Scott Township, Section 13

True-Round Barn, year built unknown
Owner when built: Unknown
Architect/Builder: Unknown

Cement staves held together with iron bands comprise the wall structure of this hog barn. It was built the same way as one would construct a cement stave silo. A cone-shaped roof shelters the livestock within.

Photo: Frank Hunter, 1979

96. MADISON COUNTY, Scott Township, Section 24

True-Round Barn, year built unknown
Owner when built: Unknown
Architect/Builder: Unknown

A hog barn with cone-type roof. Walls are of cement staves held in place by iron bands — the same method as for building a cement stave silo. The history of this barn is not known.

Photo: Frank Hunter, 1979

97. MAHASKA COUNTY, East Des Moines Township, Section 3

True-Round Barn, year built unknown
Owner when built: Unknown
Architect/Builder: Unknown

The walls are built of hollow clay tile, on

which rests a two-pitch gambrel self-supporting roof with wood shingles. Main entry doors are located on both east and west sides of the barn.

Photo: Lowell J. Soike, 1982

98. MARION COUNTY, Franklin Township, Section 16

Octagon Barn, year built unknown
Owner when built: Unknown
Architect/Builder: Unknown

The eight-sided barn noted here is about 40 feet in diameter and rests upon a stone foundation. The frame is of dimension plank lumber and covering it is horizontal wood siding. The eight-section conical roof, which has asphalt shingles, supports an attractive slender wood cupola. Wood louver vents are located in the loft and cupola. The interior has pie-shaped box stalls surrounding a central open area in which hay or feed is brought down from the loft for distribution. The barn is no longer in use.

Photo: Lowell Soike, 1982

99. MARION COUNTY, Washington Township, Section 12

True-Round Barn, 1911
Owner when built: A.G. James
Architect/Builder: Unknown

A one-story wing surrounds four-fifths of the barn, and the remainder is taken up with a one and one-half story wing shed. Horizontal shiplap siding covers the walls of the wing, shed, and barn alike. The two-pitch gambrel roof is wood shingled, with a small metal aerator on top. Diameter of the barn is 76 feet. Inside is a 14-foot diameter cement stave silo, and the remainder of the interior space is laid out following the same circular construction. Feed bunks are attached to the walls of corn and grain cribs that are built against the barn's outer wall. The shed on the south side is for horses. Featured in Wilson L. Wells, Barns in the U.S.A. (San Diego, California: Acme Printing Co., 1976).

Photo: Frank Hunter, 1979

100. MARSHALL COUNTY, State Center Township, Section 20

True-Round Barn, 1919
Owner when built: Henry A. Dobbin
Architect/Builder: Gordon-Van Tine "Barrel Barn No. 214" design

That this "Barrel Barn" plan came from Gordon-Van Tine Company, a Davenport manufacturer of pre-cut mail-order barns, is evident from the name of the company stamped on lumber inside the barn. Henry Dobbin saw the same barn built three miles east of here on the Yordy farm and decided to have one like it. It is a 60-foot diameter barn with a 12-foot diameter clay tile silo inside. The barn has a circular arrangement, with nearly one-half devoted to horse stalls and a like amount of space on the other side for cow stalls. Two box stalls are in the rear, and grain bins are located on either side of the driveway near the barn entrance. The exterior walls have vertical wood siding and the roof is of a self-supporting two-pitch gambrel type with asphalt shingles. Above is a large round cupola with louvered windows and a cone roof.

Photo: Frank Hunter, 1979

101. MARSHALL COUNTY, State Center Township, Section 25

True-Round Barn, 1919
Owner when built: W.J. Yordy
Architect/Builder: Gordon-Van Tine "Barrel Barn No. 214" design

This "barrel barn" plan was portrayed in

Gordon-Van Tine Farm Buildings 1917, a catalog of mail-order pre-cut barns available from the Davenport manufacturer. It is one of three known to have been built in the state, one of which is about three miles to the west of here. The 60-foot diameter barn contains a clay tile silo inside, and surrounding the silo is a cattle feeding area. Vertical wood siding and a two-pitch gambrel roof with asphalt shingles, crowned by a louvered window cupola and cone roof, characterize its exterior appearance.

Photo: Frank Hunter, 1979

102. MONONA COUNTY, Cooper Township, Section 33

True-Round Barn, 1921
Owner when built: Unknown
Architect/Builder: Seth Smith, carpenter

A well-known auctioneer reportedly had this barn built in 1921 in order to use it for selling his purebred cattle. The former sales barn has an open interior, vertical wood siding, and a conical roof with asphalt shingles. It now serves as a general purpose barn for cattle and hogs.

Photo: Frank Hunter, 1979

103. MONROE COUNTY, Franklin Township, Section 1

True-Round Barn, 1907-1908
Owner when built: Charles Henry Clark, Sr.
Architect/Builder: Owner designed and built

Built around a 14 x 30-foot silo in the center of the barn, Clark erected his 48-foot diameter round barn to accommodate the family's dairy herd. Feeding mangers and stanchions follow the circular arrangement inside. Doors are on the north, south, east and west. The straight conical asphalt-shingled roof extends upward at a 45-degree pitch to the cupola, which itself has a cone-shaped roof.

Photo: Lowell J. Soike, 1979

104. MONTGOMERY COUNTY, Pilot Grove Township, Section 22

True-Round Barn, 1912
Owner when built: Unknown
Architect/Builder: Unknown

Diameter of the barn is 60 feet with an 18-foot diameter wood stave silo inside. The interior space is arranged in a circular fashion around the silo. Double sliding doors are located at both front and rear sides of the barn. Exterior walls are of vertical sawed wood. The roof is of a two-pitch gambrel type with wood shingles and a small gable-roofed dormer.

Photo: Frank Hunter, 1979

105. MONTGOMERY COUNTY, Washington Township, Section 3

Sixteen-Sided Barn, 1917
Owner when built: Unknown
Architect/Builder: Sprague, builder

Little is known about the history of this barn. Its diameter is 60 feet and it has no silo in the center. The dimension plank lumber wall framing is covered with board and batten siding. Sixteen pie-shaped sections make up the two-pitch self-supporting gambrel roof. Inside, stalls are built around the entire perimeter of the exterior wall, with open space in the remainder. Originally used for hogs, the barn is presently being put to use for sheltering cattle.

Photo: Lowell J. Soike, 1982

106. OSCEOLA COUNTY, Allen Township, Section 34

87

Octagon Barn, 1906 (razed 1982)
Owner when built: Charles Lorch
Architect/Builder: Israel Bauman, carpenter

Bauman, a Mennonite carpenter, put up the original building for Charles Lorch. The owner then had a central silo built in 1912, with feed bunks around it for the cattle. Although the barn had a two-pitch, eight-section gambrel roof, which is ordinarily self-supporting, its low degree of pitch may have made necessary the resulting interior framework of posts and beams to support the roof at its midpoint.

Photo: Jan Reiste Pedley, 1982

107. OSCEOLA COUNTY, 234 Second Street, Sibley

Octagon Barn, 1916
Owner when built: E. G. Favre
Architect/Builder: Unknown

Located at the edge of Sibley, Iowa, E. G. Favre reportedly built the eight-sided building for his hog operation. The 50-foot diameter barn has a large gable-roofed rectangular extension attached on its west side. Asphalt shingles cover the eight-section conical roof and its octagon cupola, with windows at various points.

Photo: Frank Hunter, 1979

108. PAGE COUNTY, Grant Township, Section 35

True-Round Barn, ca. 1910
Owner when built: Joseph S. Tunnicliff
Architect/Builder: Unknown

Erected on a concrete block foundation, this two-story basement type barn measures 56 feet across. Horizontal 8-inch sawed wood siding wraps around the exterior walls, while above is a two-pitch gambrel roof with wood shingles and a metal aerator. The circular interior arrangement has a hay chute and two large grain bins situated in the center. The basement level has been remodeled for hog farrowing, but two stalls and the cow stanchions still remain. At one time, the basement level had an overhead track on which a metal manure carrier was suspended. Entry to the upper-level hay storage area is through large double doors on the west. High in the loft once hung a hay fork that ran on a circular track.

Photo: Frank Hunter, 1979

109. PAGE COUNTY, Harlan Township, Section 30

Octagon Barn, ca. 1882 (only foundation remains after 1960)
Owner when built: Philander Thompson
Architect/Builder: Unknown

When the roof of this barn fell in about 1960, its owner removed what remained down to the limestone foundation, installed a roof over it, and presently uses it as a hog confinement house with twenty-one farrowing pens and an open center. Features of the original bank barn design included: a 56-foot diameter with 16-foot sides; a heavy timber frame with mortise and peg construction; a basement level with sixteen stalls for horses and cows, in which animals faced the center of the barn and a driveway ran behind the stalls; and a hay chute from the loft. Oral tradition has it that the barn was a county landmark well known to early airplane pilots as a guidepost on their way. Also there is a record of 150 tons of hay having been put in it and a report that a derrick was used in the barn's construction.

Photo: 1914 postcard view by James T. Taggart, showing south facade with approach to the west entrance of the barn.

110. PAGE COUNTY, Morton Township, Section 15

Sixteen-Sided Barn, ca. 1914
Owner when built: Bill Braymen
Architect/Builder: Unknown

A large single-story barn of 90-foot diameter. Its low pitched roof is supported by a center pole and a circular series of posts from within — like a tent. Metal covers the sixteen-section conical roof, the top which has a small metal aerator. Inside, a hay space fills the center, and surrounding it are three stalls, a bin, and a loose housing area for livestock.

Photo: Frank Hunter, 1979

111. PAGE COUNTY, Valley Township, Section 16

Six-Sided Barn, 1914
Owner when built: Monroe McCoy
Architect/Builder: Unknown

Originally built as a hog sales barn it is presently used for hog raising. The interior is well lighted by a large cupola with twelve windows. The six-section roof and that of the cupola are wood shingled. Horizontal shiplap siding covers the balloon frame walls.

Photo: Frank Hunter, 1979

112. PALO ALTO COUNTY, Freedom Township, Section 19

True-Round barn, ca. 1919
Owner when built: Unknown
Architect/Builder: Unknown

The late William L. Moses of the Palo Alto County Historical Society reported in 1978 that a round barn, torn down about 1970, had been located on a farm about one-half mile northeast of Emmetsburg.

Photo not available.

113. PLYMOUTH COUNTY, America Township, Section 8

True-Round Barn, 1919
Owner when built; H.A. (Peter) Tonsfeldt
Architect/Builder: Unknown

The disproportionate size of the barn's high laminated beam, gothic curved roof gives it an unusual appearance. Peter Tonsfeldt had it built to show polled Hereford cattle on his West Urban Stock Farm and to feature his prize bull, Ito's Perfection. By building on a sheltered hill slope, Tonsfeldt gained basement floor space for stabling nurse cows and young purebred stock. In the center was an 18-foot diameter, plaster lined, wood stave silo. Around the silo in the basement level was a feed bunk and, behind it, loose stock pens. The main floor had a feed alley encircling three-fourths of the silo, followed by a manager and twenty-four cattle stanchions. On either side of the entrance drive to the silo there was a mill room, motor room, feed bin, and tool room. In September, 1981 the barn was saved from eventual demolition by moving it from the west side of LeMars to the county fairgrounds on the east side.

Photo: Frank Hunter, 1979

114. PLYMOUTH COUNTY, Johnson Township, Section 9

True-Round Barn, year built unknown
Owner when built: Unknown
Architect/Builder: Unknown

Four roof dormers placed just below the hip of this two-pitch gambrel-roofed barn distinguish its appearance. The exterior walls are constructed of hollow clay tile.

Photo: Lowell J. Soike, 1982

115. PLYMOUTH COUNTY, Meadow Township, Section 2

True-Round Barn, 1913 (destroyed by tornado, 1963)
Owner when built: J. B. Fry, Imperial Stock Farm
Architect/Builder: B. J. Diers, Granville, Iowa, designed and built

Photos, plans and details of this magnificent 90-foot round barn were published in American Carpenter and Builder 17 (April 1914), 68-69. The barn had a two-pitch gambrel roof covering the center portion of the barn with a wing shed encircling it and a curved roof over the main door entry to the second floor loft via a ramp bridge. Beneath the concrete-block ramp bridge was a stable with room for eight horses. On top of the roof rested a cupola twelve feet in diameter and six feet high. Horizontal board siding wrapped around the building's exterior walls. Inside the barn was a double circle of steel stanchions for 104 cattle, both of which had cattle facing inward with an alley running behind.

Photo: From 1914 view in *American Carpenter and Builder*

116. POCAHONTAS COUNTY, Dover Township, Section 15

True-Round Barn, year built unknown
Owner when built: Unknown
Architect/Builder: Probably Johnston Bros. Clay Works, Ft. Dodge, Iowa

One of sixteen hollow-clay-tile round barns believed built by Johnston Bros. Clay Works. The smaller dark red clay tile in the lower story and the larger tile above characterized the firm's design. A large hay dormer with projecting gable roof attaches to a wood-shingled two-pitch gambrel roof. In the center of the 60-foot diameter barn is a clay tile silo measuring 16 feet across. The building is presently in use as part of a hog raising operation.

Photo: Frank Hunter, 1979

117. POCAHONTAS COUNTY, Marshall Township, Section 35

True-Round Barn, year built unknown
Owner when built: Unknown
Architect/Builder: Unknown

This single-story clay-tile barn stands as part of an unoccupied farmstead. It has a conical roof with wood shingles.

Photo: Frank Hunter, 1979

118. POLK COUNTY, Elkhart Township, Section 31

Thirteen and one-half Sided Barn, year built unknown
Owner when built: William Lentz

Architect/Builder: Unknown

Visible to the west as travelers pass just south of the Elkhart exit of Interstate 35, this barn easily stands out on the landscape. It has an asphalt-shingled two-pitch gambrel roof, above which is a twelve-sided cupola. The exterior walls are of balloon frame construction with board and batten siding. Diameter of the barn is 56 feet. Within the barn one finds a central wood stave silo of 14-foot diameter. Around it are cattle stalls and several dairy stanchions. Part of the flooring is wood 4" x 4" set on end. In the loft overhead runs a circular hay track.

Photo: Lowell J. Soike, 1979

119. POTTAWATAMIE COUNTY, Pleasant Township, Section 6

True-Round Barn, 1926-1928
Owner when built: Richard Eckle
Architect/Builder: Ed Brown and George Robinson

Built originally for dairying, the 54-foot diameter barn was taken out of use in the 1940s. Hollow clay tile comprises the first-floor exterior walls as well as the walls of a 14-foot diameter interior silo. Horizontally applied wood siding covers the exterior walls. The roof is self-supporting, of a two-pitch gambrel type with wood shingles and a metal aerator. Within, cattle stanchions form a semi-circle around the silo, while calf pens and a separator room are against the outside walls. A milk parlor room is attached to the barn on the outside.

Photo: Frank Hunter, 1979

120. POWESHIEK COUNTY, Jackson Township, Section 4

Octagon Barn, year built unknown
Owner when built: Unknown
Architect/Builder: Unknown

This attractive eight-sided barn, with its steeply pitched octagonal cone roof punctuated by three small steeply pitched gable-roof dormers in the east, west, and south sides and by a hay dormer with a similarly pitched roof on the north, is easily visible to travelers driving east from Montezuma on Highway 85. Horizontal weather boarding is used to cover the exterior walls.

Photo: Lowell Soike, 1982

121. RINGGOLD COUNTY, Washington Township, Section 14

Nine-Sided Barn, year built unknown
Owner when built: Unknown
Architect/Builder: Plan probably based on Lloyd Z. Jones' stock barn in Illinois

This is clearly something unto itself, although an eight-sided variant is located in Warren County and a twelve-sided barn (reminiscent of this design, with its tall central section and a wing nearly surrounding it) once existed in Cedar County. The plan mirrors one for Lloyd Z. Jones' stock barn published in Wallaces' Farmer *on January 16, 1903, p. 74, and reprinted in the issues of October 25, 1907 and June 17, 1910. The central part of the barn we find here has six-sides, with a conical roof of pie-shaped sections and gable hay dormer. A nine-section wing shed is built nearly around it. The roof of the wing shed is comprised of alternating rectangular and wedge-shaped sections. In the front there are three large door entrances (for driving into the center or either side of the wing shed). Covering the exterior walls is a mixture of board and batten with vertical sawed wood siding. Diameter of the barn is 65 feet.*

Photo: Lowell J. Soike, 1979

122. SCOTT COUNTY, Blue Grass Township, Section 34

True-Round Barn, 1914
Owner when built: Charles W. Nebergall
Architect/Builder: Benton Steele, architect and contractor, Halstead, Kansas

Combines a circular interior arrangement with a driveway running through the center of the barn. Benton Steele, who erected many round barns in the Midwest, built this one during the peak years of round barn construction. Design: 56-foot diameter barn; two-pitch gambrel wood shingled roof; cupola with conical roof; walls — lower floor of clay tile and upper board and batten.

Photo: Frank Hunter, 1979

123. SCOTT COUNTY, Le Claire Township, Section 14

Octagon barn, ca. 1912
Owner when built: Unknown
Architect/Builder: Unknown

A former general-purpose barn, it is now rented for private parties. The barn measures 50 feet across and once had a 12-foot diameter silo. Poured concrete comprises the lower-story walls, while vertical wood siding covers the balloon frame structure of the store above. An asphalt shingled roof is of a self-supporting, two-pitch gambrel type constructed of eight pie-shaped sections. The interior space is open.

Photo: Frank Hunter, 1979

124. SHELBY COUNTY, Greeley Township, Section 3

Octagon Barn, year built unknown
Owner when built: Saunders
Architect/Builder: Unknown

The owner reportedly had the barn built as a sales pavilion for selling purebred hogs. Although financial reverses eventually forced him under, the octagon barn still stands as a reminder of those more prosperous days. Its condition is deteriorating, however, and little use is being made of it at present. Vertical boards cover the exterior walls. Its eight-section wood-shingled roof has a large cupola with an octagonal cone roof. These windows located in each side of the cupola's eight walls ensure that plenty of light reaches the barn's interior.

Photo: Lowell J. Soike, 1982

125. SIOUX COUNTY, Garfield Township, Section 7

True-Round Barn, year built unknown
Owner when built: Unknown
Architect/Builder: Unknown

The barn bears a close resemblance to the circular hoghouse built on the John Geiger farm in McLean County, Illinois and featured in the February 26, 1920 issue of the Breeder's Gazette. *Both have a double roof with metal roofing as well as clay-tile first-floor walls and horizontally applied wood siding around a many-windowed cupola.*

Photo: Frank Hunter, 1979

126. STORY COUNTY, Indian Creek Township, Section 5

True-Round Barn, 1916
Owner when built: Unknown
Architect/Builder: perhaps built by a man named Belcher

The conical roof, being stuccoed, gives an interesting visual effect, as does the clay tile cupola with its ring of small windows. Clay tile walls extend the entire height of this 50-foot diameter barn. Originally used as a dairying and general purpose barn, it now houses the family horse and dog.

Photo: Lowell J. Soike, 1979

127. STORY COUNTY, Indian Creek Township, Section 6

Octagon Barn, ca. 1880s
Owner when built: Unknown
Architect/Builder: Unknown

The barn's appearance mirrors, and probably derives from the plan of Lorenzo Coffin's Webster County barn (1867) that the Iowa Homestead *publicized in a January 1883 issue. It has the same modified hip-roof form and non-circular interior arrangement, along with split-level basement and ramp upper-level entries. Diameter of the eight-sided barn is about 70 feet, each side being 28 feet across. The heavy timber frame with mortise and tenon connections has vertical board and batten siding. Most of the basement level is devoted to open livestock housing.*

Photo: Lowell J. Soike, 1979

128. STORY COUNTY, Indian Creek Township, Section 27

True-Round Barn, year built unknown (torn down, 1960s)
Owner when built: Unknown
Architect/Builder: Unknown

A round barn with walls of clay tile construction once stood here, reports Joseph Tiffany, a former resident of the locality. It was torn down, he recalls, in the early 1960s.

No photo available

129. STORY COUNTY, Palestine Township, Section 9

Octagon Barn, year built unknown (removed between 1968 and 1980)
Owner when built: Unknown
Architect/Builder: Unknown

The modified hip roof of this barn marks it as one probably derivative of the plan for Lorenzo Coffin's 1867 octagon barn (Webster County) that the Iowa Homestead publicized in its January 1883 issue. The only known information relating to this barn is a photocopy of a photograph contained in mail questionnaire information gathered on octagon buildings by Kent Sissel in 1968, the collection of which is on file at the Iowa State Historical Department, Office of Historic Preservation. On the back of the photocopy are the words "Mary Peitz's, So. Nevada." An on-site investigation of a farm once owned by Mary Peitzman, however, showed no such barn present.

Photo: from xerox photocopy in notes and records from Kent Sissel's study of octagon buildings in Iowa, 1968

130. TAMA COUNTY, Buckingham Township, Section 14

True-Round Barn, 1920s
Owner when built: Unknown
Architect/Builder: Probably Johnston Bros. clay tile wall design; John Ames, builder

One of sixteen hollow-clay-tile round barns believed built by, or derived from plans of, the Johnston Bros. Clay Works, Ft. Dodge, Iowa. This is evident by the smaller dark red clay tile in the lower story and the larger tile above that characterized the firm's round

barn design. A hollow-clay-tile silo is in the middle of the 50-foot diameter barn and the interior space is arranged around it. The two-pitch gambrel roof is unusual, being constructed in its lower half of trapezoidal sections set at a steep pitch with an upper half of low pitch that extends from the hip to the metal aerator at the top. A write-up on the barn is contained in Wilson L. Wells, Barns in the U.S.A. (San Diego, California Acme Printing Co., 1976).

Photo: Lowell J. Soike, 1979

131. TAMA COUNTY, Clark Township, Section 1

True-Round Barn, 1917
Owner when built: Unknown
Architect/Builder: Probably Johnston Bros. Clay Works design; installed by a Sioux City crew

One of sixteen hollow-clay-tile barns believed built by, or derived from plans of, the Johnston Bros. Clay Works, Ft. Dodge, Iowa. An earmark of the firms's design was the use of their smaller-size dark red tile in the lower story and a larger size tile above. Features of the barn include a long rectangular addition of clay tile, a 16-foot diameter clay tile silo, a conical roof with asphalt shingles, and small-gable roof dormer. Diameter of the barn is 66-feet. The owner had the roof rebuilt in 1965, but shortly thereafter took the barn out of use.

Photo: Frank Hunter, 1979

132. TAMA COUNTY, Perry Township, Section 9

True-Round Barn, 1917
Owner when built: J. W. Young
Architect/Builder: Owner, assisted by Joe Seda, carpenter

First Young built the hollow-clay-tile silo and then, two years later, built a clay tile barn around it — the idea being to have an enclosed structure for feeding silage to his cattle from bunks around the silo. Diameter of the barn is 65 feet, and the silo is 18 feet across by 45 feet high. A windstorm took the metal roof off the silo in 1977. Asphalt shingles were applied in place of the wood shingles about 1971.

Photo: Lowell J. Soike, 1979

133. TAYLOR COUNTY, Grant Township, Section 5

True-Round Barn, ca. 1899
Owner when built: J. E. Cameron
Architect/Builder: Owner built

This is perhaps the earliest true-round barn in Iowa. The roof is noteworthy in that, being a straight conical type without interior posts to support it at the middle, the roof's longevity must in part be due to the steep pitch that relieves weight on its rafters. The barn measures about 100 feet across, with walls of board and batten siding and a wood-shingled roof crowned by a large round cupola. A set of main doors at both east and west sides allows for a driveway through the center. On each side are two grain bins, and behind them is a manger built in a semi-circle. An overhead track for a manure carrier runs behind the manger.

Photo: Lowell J. Soike, 1979

134. TAYLOR COUNTY, Polk Township, Section 12

Nine-Sided Barn, year built unknown
Owner when built: Miligan
Architect/Builder: Unknown

Originally built for silage and cattle feeding, the barn is now used only for storage. The clay tile silo is 18 feet in diameter. A wing shed frame of dimension plank lumber covered with board and batten siding extends around two-thirds of the silo. The conical roof is constructed of nine sections and has asphalt shingles.

Photo: Frank Hunter, 1979

135. UNION COUNTY, Highland Township, Section 20

True-Round Barn, 1908
Owner when built: Reid
Architect/Builder: Unknown

A dairyman named Reid had this 50-foot diameter barn built with a driveway running through the center. On each side of the drive at the center is a granary. Around one bin, in semi-circular fashion, there are twelve dairy cow stanchions and two box stalls, while there are five horse stalls around the second grain bin in the other half. The balloon frame walls have board and batten siding. Above, a two-pitch gambrel roof has wood shingles and, at its apex a circular cupola with louvered windows and cone roof.

Photo: Lowell J. Soike, 1979

136. VAN BUREN COUNTY, Des Moines Township, Section 20

True-Round Barn, 1917-1919
Owner when built: Frank Silvers
Architect/Builder: Alva Hunt, builder from Pulaski

When built, the Silvers sales pavilion at his Wickfield farm served what was claimed to be the largest Hampshire hog farm in the world and could reportedly feed 1500 hogs at one time. Walls of this 50-foot diameter barn are of hollow clay tile but it is the two-pitch gambrel roof with its eight dormers on the lower part and three on the upper that give special interest to the barn. The second story is divided into rooms off a central round hall, while the crow's nest level above was used as a card room and social parlor. During the 1930s it operated as a private club. For many years the barn has been used simply for storage.

Photo: Frank Hunter, 1979

137. VAN BUREN COUNTY, Farmington Township, Section 35

True-Round Barn, 1925
Owner when built: Bill French
Architect/Builder: Unknown

This barn's original two-pitch gambrel roof became so deteriorated that about 1969 its owners completely replaced it with a flat metal roof. Diameter of the clay tile barn is 60 feet and that of the silo, 12 feet. The interior space is open.

Photo: Frank Hunter, 1979

138. VAN BUREN COUNTY, Village Township, Section 12

True-Round Barn, 1921
Owner when built: Frank Cramlet
Architect/Builder: Plan by Louden Machinery Co., Fairfield, Iowa

This is the only Iowa round barn known to have been designed by the architectural department at Louden Machinery Co., a provider of farm building plans and equipment. It is one of three in Iowa built with a dome roof. The basement-type barn described here is 60 feet in diameter, 65 feet high, and built to hold 75 tons of hay plus about 500 bushels of grain. Louden equipment was used throughout. It had, from the beginning, running water in the basement for cattle and horses and electric lights from a home electric plant. Stanchions in the basement are arranged in circular fashion. The ground level had machinery storage space and grain bins as well as a harness room, while the loft above held loose hay. The original dome roof collapsed about 1970 and was replaced by an asphalt-shingled cone roof with a metal cone roof on the cupola.

Photo: Frank Hunter, 1979

139. WAPELLO COUNTY, Adams Township, Section 28

Round Barn, year built unknown (destroyed by windstorm, 1981)
Owner when built: Unknown
Architect/Builder: Unknown

Neither a photo nor information about the barn's characteristics was available at the time of printing.

140. WARREN COUNTY, Otter Township, Section 25

Octagon Barn, ca. 1900
Owner when built: Nutting
Architect/Builder: Resembles plan for Lloyd Z. Jones stock barn in Illinois

This octagon barn, with its tall central section and a wing shed nearly around it, is a close relative to a nine-sided barn in Ringgold County and a 12-sided model that once stood in Cedar County. The plan approximates one published on the Illinois stock barn of Lloyd Z. Jones in Wallaces' Farmer, 28

(Jan. 16, 1903), 74, and reprinted Oct. 25, 1907 and June 17, 1910. The frame of the 54-foot diameter barn combines heavy timber with balloon framing. Vertical sawed wood covers the first floor exterior walls and shiplap the second. Eight wedge-shaped sections with asphalt shingles make up the conical roof. The interior space has a rectangular arrangement in which a central driveway is flanked on one side by grain bins and on the other by open space that was at one time divided into stalls. Its original use was for horses and dairy cattle, but now it is used for hogs.

Photo: Frank Hunter, 1979

141. WASHINGTON COUNTY, Cedar Township, Section 30

16-Sided Hog Barn, year built unknown
Owner when built: Thomas Johnson
Architect/Builder: Unknown

The barn was built for, and continues to be used as, a hog farrowing house. According to Thomas Johnson's son, it was the first building that his father put up after buying the farm. It has a concrete foundation and vertical board siding with windows in one-half of the wall sections. The barn measures 40 feet across, each of the 16 sides being 8 feet wide. The straight conical roof, with asphalt shingles and metal aerator, has two rows of windows built into its south side. Inside, a ring of posts supports the roof about midway between the center and the outer wall. Fifteen pens extend around the perimeter of the exterior wall. Exterior doors are located on the northeast and southeast sides.

Photo: Lowell J. Soike, 1982.

142. WASHINGTON COUNTY, Cedar Township, Section 17

True-Round Barn, 1915 (only ruins remain as of 1982)
Owner when built: Charles W. Stewart
Architect/Builder: Unknown

This attractive concrete-block horse barn gained some publicity when its owner contributed a photo and description of it to a July 9, 1914 issue of the Chicago Breeder's Gazette. The same photo appeared in Wallaces' Farmer. The barn held up to twenty-

four horses, and had a true-conical roof with cupola and gable-roof hay dormer with rounded projecting overhang.

Photo: From Chicago *Breeder's Gazette*, July 9, 1914

143. WAYNE COUNTY, Clay Township, Section 22

True-Round Barn, year built unknown (destroyed by fire about 1969)

Owner when built: Unknown

Architect/Builder: Unknown

A round wood barn reportedly stood on the Marvin Breuer and Henry Breuer farm until one day about 1969 when hot hay caught fire, this according to a report by the operator of a fuel oil station in Corydon in May, 1979.

No photo available

144. WAYNE COUNTY, Richman Township, Section 19

True-Round Barn, year built and demolished unknown

Owner when built: George McCulloch, M.D.

Architect/Builder: Unknown

This was the smallest of three round barns that "Doc" McCulloch had built on each of his three Richman Township farms. Nothing else is known about the barn.

Photo not available.

145. WAYNE COUNTY, Richman Township, Section 20

True-Round Barn, years built and demolished unknown

Owner when built: George McCulloch, M.D.

Architect/Builder: Unknown

This round horse barn was one of three built on each of the farms owned by "Doc" McCulloch in Richman Township. This one differed from the other two in having a foundation of cement that rose to shoulder height. Nothing else is known about the building.

Photo not available.

146. WAYNE COUNTY, Richman Township, Section 21

True-Round Barn, years built and demolished unknown

Owner when built: George McCulloch, M.D.

Architect/Builder: Unknown

This is one of three round barns that "Doc" McCulloch had erected on each of three farms owned in Richman Township. It was located one-half block south of the school at the southwestern edge of Humeston. According to local historian Clarence Blackman, the barn was used for horses, with hay storage

and horse stalls in the center and an exercise track running around the perimeter. The low pitch of the conical roof suggests that a series of interior purlin posts supported it from within. The walls had vertical board siding, with wood shingles on the roof and a cupola on top.

Photo: From Centennial Book Committee, *Humeston Centennial 100 Years, 1872-1972*, (Humeston, Iowa: Humeston New Era — Madrid Register News, 1972), p. 19

147. WAYNE COUNTY, South Fork Township, Section 27

Octagon Barn, year built unknown (destroyed by fire 1957)

Owner when built: probably T.J. Anderson

Architect/Builder: Unknown

Located at the southeast edge of Promise City, the barn had a central silo with exterior walls of vertical board construction. The eight-section roof was of a two-pitch gambrel type with wood shingles. A straight conical roof with dormer sheltered the silo.

Photo: From an undated postcard view in the Wayne County Historical Museum, Corydon, Iowa.

148. WAYNE COUNTY, Warren Township, Section 12

True-Round Barn, ca. 1912

Owner when built: Unknown

Architect/Builder: Builder was a man named Nelson

The barn was once used strictly for dairy purposes but is now used for a dairy and hog operation. It measures 50 feet in diameter and has board and batten siding with an asphalt-shingled straight conical roof. Inside there is an open pen in the center with hay and grain bins, stalls, a tack room, and nine cow stanchions built around the perimeter of the wall.

Photo: Frank Hunter, 1979

149. WEBSTER COUNTY, Douglas Township, Section 14

Octagon Barn, 1867 (collapsed 1967-1968)

Owner when built: Lorenzo S. Coffin

Architect/Builder: Owner built

Coffin built what became a prototype for a series of similar barns constructed in the 1880s. This was no doubt due to the publicity about it that appeared in the state agricultural press about 1883, especially in the lead January 1883 issue of the influential Des Moines Iowa Homestead. Distinctive features of the barn included its non-self-supported modified hip roof, the basement-type (split entry) plan, a rectangular rather than circular type of interior layout (with stalls in straight rows on either side of a central drive) vertical wood siding, and a wood cupola and gable-roof dormer.

Photo: From a 1959 color print by Eugene Newhouse, Rockwell City, Iowa

150. WEBSTER COUNTY, Otho Township, Section 7

True-Round Barn, 1910

Owner when built: Johnston Bros. Clay Works

Architect/Builder: Johnston Bros. Clay Works, Ft. Dodge, Iowa

This is a prototype hollow clay tile round barn that Johnston Bros. Clay Works built or sold in Iowa's northern counties. Sixteen have been found that have the firm's characteristic smaller clay tile in the lower story and larger tile above. Several of their barns also have the metal conical roof and gable-roof dormer shown in this barn. The Johnston Brothers reportedly built this one to advertise their product. A clay tile silo with dome roof is in the center.

Photo: Frank Hunter, 1979

151. WINNEBAGO COUNTY, Norway Township Section 7

True-Round Barn, year built unknown

Owner when built: Unknown

Architect/Builder: Probably Johnston Bros. Clay Works, Ft. Dodge, Iowa

The barn is one of sixteen hollow-clay-tile barns believed built or sold by Johnston Bros. Clay Works. The smaller dark red tile in the lower story and the larger tile above characterized the firm's design. It has an 8-section conical roof with asphalt shingles and a large

93

hay dormer with overhang above the hay door. Encircling the interior clay tile silo are dairy cow stanchions in one half and horse stalls and calf pens in the other. The barn was taken out of use in 1970.

Photo: Frank Hunter, 1979

152. WINNESHIEK COUNTY, Jackson Township, Section 8

Sixteen-Sided Barn, 1918 (removed 1982)
Owner when built: Unknown
Architect/Builder: Horky Bros., Builders

Diameter of the barn is 58 feet and inside is a rare 16-foot diameter wood stave silo. Board and batten siding cover the balloon framed walls while above is a wood shingled, two-pitch, gambrel roof comprising sixteen-pie shaped sections.

Photo: Frank Hunter, 1979

153. WINNESHIEK COUNTY, Burr Oak Township, Section 13

Octagon Barn, ca. 1880s
Owner when built: L. R. Kinney
Architect/Builder: Unknown

The look of this barn mirrors, and probably derives from, the plan of Lorenzo Coffin's 1867 barn in Webster County, which the Iowa Homestead publicized in a January 1883 issue. It has the same modified hip-roof form and non-circular interior arrangement. Each of the eight-sides measures 20 feet. The interior arrangement is rectangular. On one side of the central driveway there are eight

pens, while on the other, sheep and hog pens share space with a feed room and an old milk room. Loose hay was loaded into the loft in the center of the barn via a large wooden pulley. Two 20-foot lean-to's were added to the barn by its second owner, Mr. Nash, between 1900 and 1929.

Photo: Frank Hunter, 1979

154. WINNESHIEK COUNTY, Frankville Township, Section 14

Octagon Barn, year built unknown
Owner when built: Unknown
Architect/Builder: Unknown

This may be one of the oldest extant octagon barns in the state, but its exact history is unclear. Metal siding was put over the original shiplap horizontal siding about 1900. The interior framing is dimension plank throughout. A 1970 storm destroyed the cupola and windmill that had been on top of the barn roof. Diameter of the eight-sided building is 68 feet. The barn has a basement level that housed animals. The ground floor has a 14-foot diameter wood stave silo situated to the side of a central driveway that at one time ran all the way through the barn and down a steep incline on the other side. The eight-section conical roof was reshingled a few years ago.

Photo: Frank Hunter, 1979

155. WRIGHT COUNTY, Eagle Grove Township, Section 7

True-Round Barn, year built unknown
Owner when built: Unknown
Architect/Builder: Unknown

The history of this barn is obscure. Masonry walls rise to just beyond the window line and then horizontal shiplap siding takes over thereafter. The two-pitch self-supporting gambrel roof has a small dormer situated close to the peak near the metal aerator.

Photo: Frank Hunter, 1979

156. WRIGHT COUNTY, Troy Township, Section 10

True-Round Barn, year built unknown (torn down about 1977)
Owner when built: Unknown

Architect/Builder: Probably Johnston Bros. Clay Works, Ft. Dodge, Iowa

One of sixteen hollow-clay-tile round barns believed built or sold by Johnston Bros. Clay Works. A leading characteristic of the firm's design was the use of smaller red clay tile in the lower story and larger tile above. A straight conical roof with conical cupola rested on top of the clay tile walls. Inside of this dairy barn stood a clay tile silo.

Photo: From a 1977 color slide in a collection prepared by Lloyd Oakland entitled "Early Barns in Hamilton County," on file at the Kendall Young Library, Webster City, Iowa

157. UNLOCATED IOWA SITE

True-Round Barn
Owner when built: Unknown
Architect/Builder: Unknown

W.E. Frudden publicized this "Iowa barn built of hollow clay tile" in an article written for The Field Illustrated 26 (1916), 750, and in his book, Farm Buildings (Charles City, Iowa: The Author, 1916), p. 19. Unfortunately, he noted neither the owner's name nor the barn's location. The barn measured 60 feet across with a 16-foot diameter silo in the center. It had a straight conical roof with a metal aerator at its peak. Inside were separate horse and cow sections in the basement livestock area, while the loft floor above (reached by a ramp driveway) held mainly hay storage along with some grain bin space.

Photo: From W.E. Frudden, Farm Buildings (1916), p. 19

158. UNLOCATED IOWA SITE, three miles east of Tabor

Ten-Sided Barn, years built and demolished unknown
Owner when built: Unknown
Architect/Builder: Unknown

In 1968 the president of the Fremont County Historical Society reported that a badly deteriorated ten-sided dairy barn of wood frame construction was located three miles east of Tabor in either Miles or Fremont County.

No photo available

159. UNLOCATED IOWA SITE, near Mason City

True-Round Barn, 1912

Owner when built: Unknown

Architect/Builder: C.O. Alexander, Northern Construction Co., Mason City, designed and built

An article by C.O. Alexander entitled "A Round Clay Tile Barn," appeared in the June 1913 issue of American Carpenter and Builder. *It contains photos of the building under construction as well as a floor plan and cross-section drawings. Clay tile for the barn was manufactured by the Mason City Brick and Tile Company. The 60-foot diameter building has a 14 by 34-foot silo inside. On top of the silo is a 275-barrel water tank constructed of hollow clay tile, the design of which, Alexander reported, "has been experimented on for the past few years by the Iowa Experiment Station." The interior has a circular arrangement. One half of the floor space around the silo has stalls for twenty cows, and the remaining half has box stalls for horses.*

Photo: From C.O. Alexander, "A Round Clay Tile Barn," *American Carpenter and Builder,* 15 (June 1913), 64.

160. UNLOCATED IOWA SITE

True-Round Barn, 1911

Owner when built: Unknown

Architect/Builder: G.E. Gratke, Strawberry Point, Iowa, contractor

Photos with plans and specifications by Gratke were published as "Large Round Dairy Barn," in American Carpenter and Builder *12.*

NOTES

1. B.J. Diers, "90 Foot Round Barn," *American Carpenter and Builder* 17 (April 1914), 69.

2. Ibid., 68-69.

3. The Breeder's Gazette, *Farm Buildings* (Chicago, 1916), p.52.

4. "The Round Barn for Economy," *The Field Illustrated* 26 (1916), 750.

5. The word "round" is used throughout this paper as the generic term for barns of circular shape and barns with five or more sides of equal length. Whenever one or another of these forms is singled out for discussion, we will use the specific nomenclature of true-round or circular, hexagon, octagon, or 16-sided. This is in accord with Roger L. Welsch's use of terms in his article "Nebraska's Round Barns," *Nebraska History* 51 (Spring 1970), 48-92.

6. See Larry T. Jost, *The Round and Five-or-More Equal Sided Barns of Wisconsin* (Franklin, Wis.: Privately Printed, 1980); Stephen T. Whitney, "Round Barns," *Vermont Life* 25 (Summer 1971), 8-15; Roger L. Welsch "Nebraska's Round Barns," *Nebraska History* 51 (Spring 1970), 48-92; Doris Hood, *Fulton County's Round Barns* Rochester, Ind.: Fulton County Historical Society, 1971), p.1, Lee Hartman, "Michigan's Barns, Our Vanishing Landmarks," *Michigan Natural Resources* 45 (March-April 1976), 17-32.

7. Whether or not similar trends occurred elsewhere is hard to discern from existing literature on the subject, the most informative of which are as follows: Roger L. Welsch, "The Nebraska Round Barn," *Journal of Popular Culture* 1 (Spring 1968), 403-409; idem, "Nebraska's Round Barns," *Nebraska History* 51 (Spring 1970), 48-92; Jerry Apps and Allen Strang, "Fowler's Folly: Round and Polygonal Barns," in their *Barns of Wisconsin* (Madison, Wis.: Tamarack Press, 1977), pp. 42-48, 135; Eric Arthur and Dudley Witney, "Circular and Polygonal Barns" in *The Barn: A Vanishing Landmark in North America* (Greenwich, Conn.: New York Geographic Society, 1972), pp. 146-157; Robert-Lionel Sequin, *Les Granges de Quebec du XVIIe au XIXe siecle,* (Musee National Du Canada, 1963), pp. 82-94; Stephen T. Whitney, "Round Barns," *Vermont Life* 25 (Summer 1971), 8-15; Bertha Kitchell Whyte, "Octagonal Houses and Barns," *Wisconsin Magazine of History* 34 (Autumn 1950), 42-46; and Eric Sloane, *An Age of Barns* (New York: Ballentine Books/Random House, 1974), pp. 54-57.

8. Paul Leland Hawarth, *George Washington: Farmer* (Indianapolis: Bobbs-Merrill Company, 1915), pp. 124-125.

9. Solon Robinson, ed., *Facts For Farmers,* 2 vols. (New York: A.J. Johnson, 1868), 1: 302-303; Arthur and Witney, *The Barn,* p. 151; "The Great Shaker Barn," *Cultivator and Country Gentleman,* 20 (Oct. 9, 1862), 242.

10. "Plan of Farm Buildings for Animals," *Cultivator and Country Gentleman* 4 (Aug. 17, 1854), 108.

11. "Mr. Calvert's Barn," *Cultivator and Country Gentleman* 4 (Oct. 26, 1854), 262. See also "Riversdale" in the issue of Sept. 3, 1857, 161-162.

12. "Mr. Calvert's Farm Buildings," *Cultivator and Country Gentleman* 4 (Dec. 14, 1854), 374-375.

13. Orson Squire Fowler, *A Home for All* (New York: Fowler and Well, 1854), pp. 174-178.

14. Carl F. Schmidt, *The Octagon Fad* (Scottsville, N.Y.: Privately Printed, 1958), p. 1.

15. E.W. Stewart, "An Octagonal Barn," reprinted as a series in *National Live-Stock Journal* 9 (Feb., March, April, 1878), 52-53, 100-101, 149.

16. *Cultivator and Country Gentleman* 41 (Aug. 31, 1876), 554; *American Agriculturalist* 35 (July 1876), 258-259.

17. "Construction of Barns," in *Illustrated Annual Register of Rural Affairs* (Albany, N.Y.: Cultivator and Country Gentleman, 1878), pp. 229, 249-252.

18. *National Live-Stock Journal* 9 (Feb. 1878), 52. Later, in August 1885, the editor reported that the 1878 publication of Stewart's plan "attracted much attention, and our supply of numbers for those months was exhausted long since, except in some complete volumes kept for binding."

19. J.P. Sheldon, *Dairy Farming* (London and New York: Cassell, Petter, Gilpin and Company, ca. 1885), pp. 87-91.

20. Elliott Stewart, *Feeding Animals: A Practical Work Upon the Laws of Animal Growth Specially Applied to the Breeding and Feeding of Horses, Cattle, Dairy Cows, Sheep and Swine,* 2nd ed. (Lake View, N.Y.: Privately Printed, 1883), pp. 89-92.

21. "Octagonal Barns," *Cultivator and Country Gentleman* 49 (Aug. 14, 1884), 579.

22. An octagon barn 20 feet on a side, or 160 feet, had an approximate floor space of 1928 square feet, while a square barn 40 feet on a side had an area of only 1600 square feet, Stewart, *Feeding Animals,* p. 89.

23. Ibid.

24. Ibid.

25. For information on the better farming movement as it concerned early Iowa, see Mildred Throne, "Book Farming in Iowa," *Iowa Journal of History* 49 (April 1951), 117-142.

26. Sheldon, *Dairy Farming,* p. 91.

27. Reprinted as *Barns, Sheds and Outbuildings* (Brattleboro, Vt.: Stephen Greene Press, 1977), p. 13.

28. Ibid., p. xii.

29. *National Live-Stock Journal* 9 (March 1878), 101.

30. Lorenzo S. Coffin, "An Iowa Farm Barn: How to Build on Octagon Barn — Its Convenience and Economy," Des Moines *Iowa Homestead,* Jan. 5, 1883. See also Coffin's article, "Barns," in his "Home and Farm" column, Fort Dodge *Messenger,* Oct. 20, 1882. For biographical information on Coffin, see *History of Fort Dodge and Webster County, Iowa* 2 vols. (Chicago: The Pioneer Publishing Company, 1913), 1:148-151; *Biographical Record and Portrait Album of Webster and Hamilton Counties, Iowa* (Chicago: Lewis Publishing Company, 1888), pp. 452-454; and Earle D. Ross, "Lorenzo S. Coffin — Farmer," *The Palimpsest* 22 (Oct. 1941), 289-292.

31. Two small octagon barns in Iowa date from the early 1870s. One, built before 1875 and not extant, is illustrated in the engraved view of the J.F. Hopkins farm in Boone County shown in *A.T. Andreas' Illustrated Historical Atlas of the State of Iowa, 1875* (1875, reprinted, Iowa City: Iowa State Historical Society of Iowa, 1970), p. 317. A second one, also shown in the *Andreas Atlas,* p. 338, was on William L. McCroskey's Waveland Farm in Cedar County. Both of these octagon barns were secondary buildings that simply augmented the larger barn space being provided by rectangular barns.

32. See barn entry 109 in Appendix.

33. Mrs. James Souer, "Landmark Near Delta, An Eight-Sided Barn, No Longer Stands,"Oskaloosa *Daily Herald,* Nov. 27, 1965.

34. Ibid.

35. Des Moines *Iowa Homestead,* Dec. 29, 1882. See also the reprint of Coffin's Fort Dodge *Messenger* article in the Oct. 20, 1882 issue of the *Iowa Homestead.*

36. Coffin, "An Iowa Farm Barn," Des Moines *Iowa Homestead,* Jan. 5, 1883.

37. The substantial level of reader interest in obtaining more information about the barn is noted in Des Moines *Iowa Homestead,* Feb. 16, 1883.

38. Letter to the editor from S. Parish, Gilman, Iowa in Des Moines *Iowa Homestead,* March 16, 1883.

39. Letter to the editor from C.A. Brownson, Rockdale, Iowa in *Iowa Homestead,* March 16, 1883.

40. See barn entries 30 and 84 in Appendix.

41. West Branch *Local Record,* May 31, 1883. For biographical information on Joshua H. Secrest, see *Portrait and Biographical Record of Johnson, Poweshiek and Iowa Counties, Iowa,* (Chicago: Chapman Brothers, 1893), pp. 465-466; *Leading Events in Johnson County Iowa History: Biographical* (Cedar Rapids: Western Historical Press, 1913), pp. 196-199.

42. National Register file for Secrest-Ryan Octagonal Barn, (site no. 52-79N5W-001) Iowa State Historical Department, Office of Historic Preservation, Des Moines, Iowa. See entry 83 in Appendix.

43. See round barn entries 23, 49, 50, 56, 78, 89, 122, and 143 in Appendix.

44. *Ernst Clausing built many on farms concentrated in southeastern Ozaukee County, Wisconsin, according to Whyte, "Octagonal Houses and Barns," 43-45.*

45. "Construction of Barns," *Illustrated Annual Register of Rural Affairs* (Albany, N.Y., 1878), 8 250-252.

46. Arguments against erecting the silo inside the barn persisted through the 1890s and beyond. See "Round Dairy Barn and Silo," *Cultivator and Country Gentleman,* (Feb. 22, 1894), 152; "The Circular Cow-Barn: A More Practical Structure Proposed," *Country Gentleman,* (Dec. 15, 1898), 992; F.M. White and D.I. Griffith, Barns for Wisconsin Dairy Farms, Wisconsin Agricultural Experiment Station, Bulletin 266 (Madison, Wis., 1916), p.6.

47. For a comparative perspective in an adjoining state see Roger Welsch, "Nebraska's Round Barns."

48. Joseph E. Wing, "An Octagon Cattle Barn," *Breeder's Gazette,* July 2, 1902.

49. F.H. King, The Construction of Silos, University of Wisconsin Agricultural Experiment Station, Bulletin 28 (Madison, Wis., 1891). In this study of different types of silos then is use (including the round wood-stave silo) in four midwestern states, King presented what became known as the Wisconsin, or King, all-wood round silo. The King silo achieved widespread popularity during the next few years. By his writings, with their easy-to-understand descriptions of how to build the silo, his reputation as an agricultural engineer, his advocacy of round silos through field demonstration and "ensilage schools," he contributed, perhaps more than anyone else to establishing the round silo's supremacy. The experiment stations elsewhere began to undertake parallel research. Although in 1891 King still approved of the square silo, the prominence given in the bulletin to illustrating his all-wood round silo obscured that fact. Successive bulletins that elaborated and refined his ideas appeared in 1893, 1897, and 1900 and in editions of his textbook, the *Physics of Agriculture.* Within only a few years the free-standing cylindrical silo had effectively displaced its inferior cousins — the pit silo and the short, squat, rectangular or square silo — and in the process altered the look and the operation of America's dairy farms. See Eric E. Lampard, *The Rise of the Dairy Industry in Wisconsin: A Study of Agricultural Change, 1820-1920* (Madison: State Historical Society of Wisconsin, 1963), p. 161; N.S. Fish, "The History of the Silo in Wisconsin," *Wisconsin Magazine of History* 8 (Dec. 1924), *167-168;*

National Silo Association, The History of Concrete Tower Silos and the Silo Association (Waterloo: Privately Printed, 1977), pp. 14-16; Tamara Tieman, "The Silo in Iowa: A Literature Survey," Preliminary Farm structure report prepared for the Iowa State Historical Department, Office of Historic Preservation, 1977, pp. 5-6, 14-16.

50. F.H. King, "Plan of a Barn for a Dairy Farm," University of Wisconsin Agricultural Experiment Station *Seventh Annual Report* (Madison, Wis., 1890), 183.

51. Ibid.

52. Fort Atkinson (Wis.) *Hoard's Dairyman*, April 19, 1895; Mar. 26, 1897.

53. J.H. Sanders, *Practical Hints About Barn Building* (Chicago: J.S. Sanders Publishing Co., 1893), pp. 100-101; *Breeder's Gazette*, April 7, 1897; Breeder's Gazette, *Farm Building*, new and enlarged edition (Chicago: The Breeder's Gazette, 1916), pp. 126, 129; F.H. King, *A Text Book of the Physics of Agriculture*, 6th ed. (Madison, Wis.: The Author, 1914), pp. 341-342. The original edition of King's book appeared in 1900, and farmers could purchase copies of the book from the office of *Hoard's Dairyman*.

54. H.E. Crouch, "Round Barns at Illinois Experiment Station," *Hoard's Dairyman*, Mar. 27, 1914.

55. Henry A. Wallace, "Dairy Work at the University of Illinois," *Wallaces' Farmer*, Nov. 24, 1911. Economy of the Round Dairy Barn, University of Illinois Agricultural Experiment Station, Bulletin 143 (Urbana, Ill., 1910); Wilber J. Fraser, The Round Barn, University of Illinois Agricultural Experiment Station, Circular 230 (Urbana, Ill., 1918).

56. Henry Giese, "Trends in Farm Structures," in *A Century of Farming in Iowa 1846-1946* (Ames: Iowa State College Press, 1946), p. 255.

57. Iowa Experiment Station Dairy Barn Plan No. D-1, identified in List of Farm Buildings Plans, Iowa College of Agriculture Extension Department, Bulletin 33 (Ames, 1916), p. 3. We were unable to locate a copy of the plan.

58. C.O. Alexander, "A Round Clay Tile Barn," *American Carpenter and Builder* 15 (June 1913), 64.

59. See Joseph E. Wing, "An Iowa Round Barn," *Breeder's Gazette*, 48 (August 16, 1905), 273-274; idem. *Farm Buildings.* New enlarged edition (Chicago, 1916), pp. 51-52.

60. C.B. Reynolds' letter to the editor printed as "Another Round Barn," *Breeder's Gazette* 68 (Sept. 13, 1905), 466.

61. Wing, "An Iowa Round Barn," 273.

62. Ibid.

63. Another instance of replacing an original conical roof with a gambrel one occurred with the Hart round barn in Postville, listed as entry 9 in Appendix.

64. Wilson L. Wells, *Barns In the U.S.A.* (San Diego, Calif.: Acme Printing Co., 1976). See also W.E. Frudden, *Farm Buildings: How to Build Them* (Charles City, Iowa: The Author, 1916), p.15.

65. The smallest was forty-eight feet and the largest seventy-two, but sixty feet in diameter was most common.

66. C.O. Alexander, "A Round Clay Tile Barn," *American Carpenter and Builder* 15 (June 1913), 64-65.

67. The leading producers of clay tile were in Webster, Cerro Gordo, and Polk counties. Smaller clay works could be found in many other counties, and the Ames Experiment Station claimed that tile could be shipped cheaply anywhere in the state.

68. William A. Radford, ed., *Radford's Practical Barn Plans* (Chicago: Radford Architectural Company, 1909); Louden Machinery Company, *Louden Barn Plans* (Fairfield, Iowa: Louden Machinery Co., 1915).

69. Fairfield *Daily Ledger-Journal*, April 25, 1923. See barn entry 138 in Appendix.

70. Secretary of Permanent Buildings Society to B.J. Holtkamp, Feb. 22, 1917; and C.A. Wilson of Permanent Buildings Society to Holtkamp, March 27, 1917, inventory files, Iowa State Historical Department, Office of Historic Preservation, Des Moines, Iowa. See barn entry 68 in Appendix.

71. Matt L. King, "An Umbrella for the Cattle," *American Carpenter and Builder* 23 (June 1917), 54-55.

72. G.E. Gratke, "Large Round Dairy Barn," *American Carpenter and Builder* 12 (Dec. 1911), 62-63. See barn entry 160 in Appendix.

73. B.J. Diers, "90-Foot Round Barn," *American Carpenter and Builder* 17 (April 1914), 68-69.

74. W.E. Frudden, "A Round Dairy Barn of Hollow Tile," *Building Age* (June 1915), 27-28. He also featured the barn in his book, *Farm Buildings*, p.17. See round barn entry 55 in Appendix.

75. Frudden, "A Round Dairy Barn," 27.

76. Benton Steele, "A Modern Circular Barn," *Hoard's Dairyman*, Aug. 19, 1910.

77. *Hoard's Dairyman*, March 1, 1907; April 3, 1908; Aug. 19, 1910; *Kimball's Dairy Farmer* June 15, Nov. 15, 1912; Sept 1, 1914. See also Breeder's Gazette, *Farm Buildings*, pp. 27-28, and *Breeder's Gazette*, March 4, 1903; Dec. 20, 1923. The information about Nebergall visiting a Steele-built barn near Casey was reported to us by his grandson, Donald Nebergall. The Hollenbeck barn is noted in entry 2 of Appendix.

78. Steele to Nebergall, Jan. 7, 1915, inventory files, Iowa State Historical Department, Office of Historic Preservation, Des Moines, Iowa. See barn entry 122 in Appendix.

79. Ibid.

80. See round barn entry 131 in Appendix.

81. Damon Ohlerking, *A Common Beginning* (Fort Dodge, Iowa: MIDAS Council of Governments, 1975), p. 105. See barn entry 150 in Appendix.

82. See barn entries 13, 14, and 15 in Appendix.

83. *Gordon-Van Tine Farm Buildings* (catalog) (Davenport, Iowa: Gordon-Van Tine Company, 1917), p. 5.

84. Ibid., p. 46.

85. Ibid., p. 47.

86. Ibid., p. 6.

87. Ibid., p. 47.

88. See barn entries 100 and 101 in Appendix.

89. See barn entry 91 in Appendix.

90. See barn entry 44 in Appendix.

91. See barn entry 34 in Appendix.

92. J.H. Brown, "Dairy Barns and Lawns on a Modern Dairy Farm," *Hoard's Dairyman,* May 7, 1909.

93. S.C. Burt, "Advantages and Disadvantages of the Round Barn: First One Built 25 Years Ago," Huntington *Indiana Farmer's Guide,* Nov. 9, 1918.

94. "Round or Rectangular Barns," *Hoard's Dairyman,* Sept. 4, 1908.

95. I.W. Dickerson, "Round Versus Rectangular Barns," in his "Farm Engineering" column, Des Moines *Wallaces' Farmer,* Feb. 22, 1918.

96. "The Round Dairy Barn," *Iowa Homestead,* April 29, 1909.

97. Ibid.

98. Ibid.

99. E.L.D. Seymour, ed., *Farm Knowledge* (Garden City, N.Y.: Doubleday, Page and Co., 1918), 3: 414.

100. C.F. Doane, "Round Barns Not Practical," *Hoard's Dairyman,* Feb. 20, 1914. See also his "Round Barn Handicaps," *Country Gentleman* 77 (Sept. 14, 1912), 26.

101. White and Griffith, "Barns for Wisconsin," p.6.

102. Oscar Gunderson's letter to the editor, "A Boost for the Round Barn," *Country Gentleman* 82 (May 19, 1917), 19.

103. Issac Phillips Roberts, *The Farmstead,* 7th ed. (New York: Macmillan Company, 1914), p. 255.

104. Seymour, *Farm Knowledge,* p. 414.

105. Letter to the editor from A.E. Smith, *Hoard's Dairyman,* Feb. 28, 1908.

106. W.A. Foster and R.S. Stephensen, *Cattle Feeding Barns and Shelters,* Iowa State College of Agriculture and Mechanic Arts Agricultural Experiment Station, Circular 74 (Ames, 1922); W.A. Foster and Earl Weaver, Dairy Barns and Equipment, Iowa State College of Agriculture and Mechanic Arts, Agricultural Experiment Station, Circular 93 (Ames, 1925).

107. Fred C. Fenton, "A Round Dairy Barn: Dairy Farmer Plan No. 0." Des Moines *Dairy Farmer,* formerly *Kimball's Dairy Farmer,* (Aug. 1927), 13.

108. Burt, "Advantages and Disadvantages."

109. Doon *Press,* Feb. 1, 1973.

110. What follows is based in the account of Dick and Glada Koerselman, distilled from their stories in the LeMars *Sentinel,* which appears as "LeMars Round Barn — Its Move and Memories" in the Spring 1982 issue of *The Bracket,* the Office of Historic Preservation's newsletter. Also see round barn entry 113 in Appendix.

BIBLIOGRAPHY

Agricultural Newspapers/Journals

Albany (N.Y.) *Cultivator and Country Gentleman.* 1854-1930.

Burt, S.C. "Advantages and Disadvantages of the Round Barn: First One Built 25 Years Ago." Huntington *Indiana Farmer's Guide* 30 (1918):5.

Chicago (Ill.) *Breeder's Gazette.* 1895-1910.

Chicago (Ill.) *National Live-Stock Journal.* 1872-1888.

Chicago (Ill.) *Prairie Farmer.* 1869-1872, 1885-1886, 1888, 1916, 1919, 1921-1922, 1925.

Coffin, Lorenzo S. "Barns." Fort Dodge *Messenger,* Oct. 20, 1882.

Des Moines (Iowa) *Homestead.* 1865-1916.

Des Moines (Iowa) *Wallaces' Farmer.* 1893-1930.

Ft. Atkinson (Wis.) *Hoard's Dairyman.* 1891-1920.

New York City (N.Y.) *American Agriculturalist.* 1860-1886.

"Round Barn for Economy." *Field Illustrated* 26 (1916): 270.

"Round Barn is Farm Landmark." Fairfield (Iowa) *Daily Ledger-Journal,* April 25, 1923.

Souer, Mrs. James. "Landmark Near Delta, An Eight-Sided Barn, Nor Longer Stands." Oskaloosa *Daily Herald,* November 27, 1965.

"Those Curious Round Barns." Doon (Iowa) *Press,* February 1, 1973.

Waterloo (Iowa) *Kimball's Dairy Farmer.* 1911-1925.

West Branch (Iowa) *Local Record,* May 31,1883.

General Works

Apps, Jerry, and Strang, Allen. *Barns of Wisconsin.* Madison, Wis.: Tamarack Press, 1977.

Arthur, Eric and Witney, Dudley. *The Barn: A Vanishing Landmark in North America.* Greenwich, Conn.: New York Geographic Society Ltd., 1972.

A. T. Andreas' Illustrated Historical Atlas of the State of Iowa, 1875. 1875. Reprint. Iowa City: Iowa State Historical Society, 1970.

Biographical Record and Portrait Album of Webster and Hamilton Counties, Iowa. Chicago: Lewis Publishing Company, 1888.

Breeder's Gazette. *Farm Buildings.* Chicago: Breeder's Gazette, 1916.

Britt Centennial Committee. *Recollections of Britt, Iowa 1878-1978.* Britt, Iowa: Britt Centennial Committee, 1978.

Cedar County Historical Society. *Cedar County Historical Review.* Tipton, Iowa: Cedar County Historical Society, 1980.

Centennial History Book Committee. *Centennial History Book of Anita: A Century Unfolds, 1875-1975.* Anita, Iowa: Anita Centennial Committee, 1975.

Centennial Book Committee. *Humeston Centennial 100 Years, 1872-1972.* Humeston, Iowa: Humeston New Era-Madrid Register News, 1972.

Ekblaw, K.J.T. *Farm Structures.* New York: Macmillan Company, 1916.

Foster, W.A. and Carter, Deane G. *Farm Buildings.* New York: John Wiley and Sons, Inc., 1922.

Foster, W.A. and Weaver, Earl. *Dairy Barns and Equipment.* Iowa State College of Agriculture and Mechanic Arts Agricultural Experiment Station Circular 93. Ames, 1925.

Foster, W.A. and R.S. Stephensen. *Cattle Feeding Barns and Shelters.* Iowa State College of Agriculture and Mechanic Arts Agricultural Experiment Station Circular 74. Ames, 1922.

Fowler, Orson Squire. *A Home for All; or, The Gravel Wall and Octagon Mode of Building.* New York: Fowler and Wells, 1854.

Fraser, Wilber J. *Economy of the Round Dairy Barn.* University of Illinois Agricultural Experiment Station Bulletin 143. Urbana, Ill., 1910.

Fraser, Wilber J. *The Round Barn.* University of Illinois Agricultural Experiment Station Circular 230. Urbana, Ill., 1918.

Frudden, W.E. *Farm Buildings: How to Build Them.* Charles City, Iowa: Privately Printed, 1916.

Giese, Henry. "Trends in Farm Structures." In *A Century of Farming in Iowa 1846-1946.* Ames: Iowa State College Press, 1946.

Gordon-Van Tine Company. *Gordon-Van Tine Farm Buildings.* Davenport, Iowa: Gordon-Van Tine Company, 1917.

Gordon-Van Tine Company. *Gordon Van Tine Farm Buildings.* Davenport, Iowa: Gordon-Van Tine Company, 1926.

Halstad, Byron D. *Barns, Sheds and Outbuildings.* 1881. Reprint. Brattleboro, Vt.: Stephen Greene Press, 1977.

Hawarth, Paul Leland. *George Washington: Farmer.* Indianapolis: Bobbs-Merrill Company, 1915.

History of Fort Dodge and Webster County, Iowa. Vol. I. Chicago: Pioneer Publishing Company, 1913.

Hood, Doris. *Fulton County's Round Barns.* Rochester, Ind.: Fulton County Historical Society, 1971.

Illustrated Annual Register of Rural Affairs. Albany, N.Y.: Cultivator and Country Gentleman, 1878.

Jost, Larry T. *The Round and Five-or-More Equal Sided Barns of Wisconsin.* Franklin, Wis.: Privately Printed, 1980.

King, Franklin H. *A Textbook of the Physics of Agriculture.* 6th ed. Madison, Wis.: Privately Printed, 1914.

King, F.H. *The Construction of Silos.* University of Wisconsin Agricultural Experiment Station Bulletin 28. Madison, Wis., 1891.

King, F.H. *Plan of a Barn for a Dairy Farm.* University of Wisconsin Agricultural Experiment Station Seventh Annual Report. Madison, Wis., 1890.

Lampard, Eric E. *The Rise of the Dairy Industry in Wisconsin: A Study of Agricultural Change 1820-1920.* Madison: State Historical Society of Wisconsin, 1963.

Leading Events in Johnson County History: Biographical. Cedar Rapids, Iowa: Western Historical Press, 1913.

List of Farm Buildings Plans. Iowa College of Agriculture Extension Department Bulletin 23. Ames, 1916.

Louden Machinery Company. *Louden Barn Plans.* Fairfield, Iowa: Louden Machinery Co., 1915.

National Silo Association. *The History of Concrete Tower Silos and the Silo Association.* Waterloo, Iowa: Privately Printed, 1977.

Ohlerking, Damon. *A Common Beginning.* Fort Dodge, Iowa: MIDAS Council of Governments, 1975.

Portrait and Biographical Record of Johnson, Poweshiek and Iowa Counties, Iowa. Chicago: Chapman Brothers, 1893.

Radford, William A., ed. *Radford's Practical Barn Plans.* Chicago: Radford Architectural Company, 1909.

Roberts, Issac Phillips. *The Farmstead.* 7th ed. New York: Macmillan Publishing Co., Inc., 1914.

Robinson, Solon, ed. *Facts For Farmers.* 2 vols. New York: A.J. Johnson, 1868.

Sanders, J.H. *Practical Hints About Barn Building.* Chicago: J.H. Sanders Publishing Company, 1893.

Schmidt, Carl F. *The Octagon Fad.* Scottsville, N.Y.: Privately Printed, 1958.

Sequin, Robert-Lionel. *Les Granges de Quebec du X'VIIe au XIXe siecle.* Musee National Du Canada, Bulletin no. 192. Ottawa: Ministere du Nord Canadien et des Ressources Nationales, 1963.

Seymour, E.L.D. *Farm Knowledge.* vol. 3. Garden City, N.Y.: Doubleday, Page and Company, 1918.

Shearer, Herbert A. *Farm Buildings.* Chicago: Frederick J. Drake & Co., 1917.

Sheldon, J.P. *Dairy Farming.* London and New York: Cassell, Petter, Gilpin and Company, ca. 1885.

Sloan, Eric. *An Age of Barns.* New York: Random House, Inc., Ballantine Books, 1974.

Stewart, Elliott. *Feeding Animals: A Practical Work Upon the Laws of Animal Growth Specially Applied to the Rearing and Feeding of Horses, Cattle, Dairy Cows, Sheep and Swine.* 2d ed. Lake View, N.Y.: Privately Printed, 1883.

Tieman, Tamara. "The Silo in Iowa: A Literature Survey." Preliminary farm structure report prepared for the Iowa State Historical Department, Office of Historic Preservation, 1977.

Wells, Wilson L. *Barns in the U.S.A.* San Diego, Califo.: Acme Printing Co., 1976.

White, F.M. and Griffith, D.I. *Barns for Wisconsin Dairy Farms.* Wisconsin Agricultural Experiment Station Bulletin 266. Madison, Wis., 1916.

Articles

Alexander, C.O. "A Round Clay Tile Barn." *American Carpenter and Builder* 15 (1913): 64-65.

Diers, B.J. "90 Foot Round Barn." *American Carpenter and Builder* 17 (1914): 68-69.

Fish, N.S. "The History of the Silo in Wisconsin." *Wisconsin Magazine of History* 8 (1924): 167-168.

Frudden, W.E. "A Round Dairy Barn of Hollow Tile." *Building Age* (1915): 27-28.

Gratke, G.E. "Large Round Dairy Barn." *American Carpenter and Builder* 17 (1914): 68-69.

Hartman, Lee. "Michigan Barns, Our Vanishing Landmarks", *Michigan Natural Resources.* 45 (1976): 17-32.

King, Matt L. "An Umbrella for the Cattle." *American Carpenter and Builder* 23 (1917), 54-55.

Koerselman, Dick and Gladas. "LeMars Round Barn — Its Move and Memories." *The Bracket* (Spring 1982).

Perrin, Richard W.E. "Circle and Polygon in Wisconsin Architecture: Early Structures of Unconventional Design." *Wisconsin Magazine of History* 47 (1963): 50-58.

Ross, Earle D. "Lorenzo S. Coffin — Farmer." *The Palimpsest* 22 (1941): 289-292.

Throne, Mildred. "'Book Farming' in Iowa." *Iowa Journal of History* 49 (1951): 117-142.

Welsch, Roger L. "The Nebraska Round Barn." *Journal of Popular Culture* 1 (19680: 403-409.

Welsch, Roger L. "Nebraska's Round Barns." *Nebraska History* 51 (1970): 49-92.

Westerfield, Richard. "There's Character in Barns." *Iowan* 12 (1964): 36-40.

Whitney, Stephen T. "Round Barns." *Vermont Life* 25 (1971): 8-15.

Whyte, Bertha Kitchell. "Octagonal Houses and Barns." *Wisconsin Magazine of History* 34 (1950): 42-46.

INDEX TO CATALOG
BY SELECTED BUILDING CHARACTERISTICS

A. Barn Types
  1. Octagon Barns (40 total entries)
     1, 21, 23, 25, 27, 29, 30, 32, 33, 38, 43, 45, 52, 53, 59,
     75, 78, 79, 80, 82, 83, 84, 86, 87, 90, 93, 98, 106, 107,
     109, 120, 123, 124, 147, 129, 140, 147, 149, 153, 154

  2. True-Round Barns (91 total entries)
     2, 3, 4, 5, 7, 8, 9, 11, 12, 13, 14, 15, 16, 17, 18, 19, 20,
     24, 28, 36, 39, 40, 41, 42, 44, 46, 47, 48, 49, 50, 55, 56,
     57, 58, 62, 63, 64, 65, 66, 68, 69, 71, 72, 73, 74, 85, 89,
     91, 92, 95, 96, 97, 99, 100, 101, 102, 103, 104, 108, 112,
     113, 114, 115, 116, 119, 122, 125, 126, 128, 130, 131,
     132, 133, 135, 136, 137, 138, 141, 142, 143, 144, 145,
     146, 148, 150, 151, 155, 156, 157, 159, 160

  3. Other Polygonal Barns (28 total entries)
     6, 10, 22, 26, 31, 34, 35, 37, 51, 54, 60, 61, 67, 70, 76,
     77, 81, 88, 94, 105, 110, 111, 118, 121, 134, 141, 152,
     158

B. Roof Types
  1. Sectional Cone Roofs (40 total entries)
     1, 6, 10, 21, 22, 23, 25, 27, 31, 32, 33, 35, 45, 51, 52, 53,
     60, 61, 75, 76, 78, 79, 80, 82, 83, 86, 93, 94, 98, 109,
     110, 111, 120, 121, 124, 125, 134, 141, 152, 158

  2. Straight Cone Roof (28 total entries)
     13, 14, 15, 26, 39, 42, 44, 48, 50, 63, 69, 73, 92, 95, 96,
     102, 102, 117, 126, 131, 133, 138, 141, 146, 148, 150,
     156, 157

  3. Modified Hip Roof (8 total entries)
     30, 59, 84, 87, 127, 129,

  4. Dome Roof (5 total entries)
     2, 28, 41, 113, 138

  5. Gambrel Roof (67 total entries)
     3, 4, 5, 7, 8, 9, 11, 12, 16, 17, 18, 19, 20, 24, 34, 36, 37,
     40, 43, 46, 47, 54, 55, 56, 58, 62, 64, 65, 66, 67, 68, 70,
     71, 72, 74, 81, 85, 88, 89, 90, 91, 97, 99, 100, 101, 104,
     105, 106, 108, 114, 115, 116, 118, 119, 122, 123, 130,
     132, 135, 136, 137, 142, 147, 152, 155, 159, 160

  6. Other Roof Types (4 total entries)
     38, 57, 77, 137

C. Walls
  1. Horizontal Siding (34 total entries)
     1, 7, 9, 23, 26, 27, 34, 52, 53, 59, 60, 61, 67, 75, 77, 79,
     80, 82, 86, 89, 90, 92, 93, 98, 99, 108, 111, 113, 115,
     119, 120, 154, 155, 160

  2. Vertical Siding (62 total entries)
     3, 4, 5, 6, 8, 10, 11, 20, 21, 22, 25, 28, 30, 31, 32, 35, 37,
     38, 40, 44, 45, 49, 51, 54, 70, 72, 73, 76, 78, 82, 83, 84,
     85, 87, 88, 91, 100, 101, 102, 103, 104, 105, 106, 109,
     110, 118, 121, 122, 123, 124, 127, 129, 133, 134, 135,
     150, 151, 146, 147, 148, 149, 152, 153

  3. Hollow-Clay Tile (48 total entries)
     2, 12, 13, 14, 15, 16, 17, 18, 19, 24, 36, 39, 42, 46, 47,
     48, 50, 55, 56, 57, 62, 63, 64, 65, 66, 68, 71, 74, 97, 114,
     116, 117, 119, 122, 125, 126, 128, 130, 131, 132, 136,
     137, 138, 150, 151, 156, 160

  4. Cement Stave and Concrete (7 total entries)
     58, 69, 94 95, 96, 142, 155

  5. Other (3 total entries)
     41, 43, 154

INDEX

PHOTOGRAPH CREDITS

1. Photo reproduced by permission from Wehner, Nowysz, Pattschull & Pfiffner Architects, *Woodlawn Pope-Leighey House: Comprehensive Development Plan* (Iowa City, Ia.: Privately Printed, 1981), p. 18.
2. Plan reproduced by permission from Paul Leland Haworth, *George Washington: Farmer,* Indianapolis, Ind.: Bobbs-Merrill, 1915, facing p. 24.
3. Drawing of barn reproduced from Chicago *National Live-Stock Journal,* 9 (Feb. 1878), 59.
4. Floor plan from Albany *Cultivator and Country Gentleman,* 49 (Aug. 14, 1884), 679.
5. Photo of Stewart from *The Town of Evans* [New York] *Sesqui-Centennial* booklet, n.d.
6. Engraving from *Biographical Record and Portrait Album of Webster and Hamilton Counties, Iowa* (Chicago: Lewis Publishing Company, 1888), facing p. 453.
7. From a 1959 color snapshot by Eugene Newhouse.
8. From an engraving in *A. T. Andreas' Illustrated Historical Atlas of the State of Iowa* (1875, reprinted, Iowa City: Iowa State Historical Society, 1970), p. 317.
9. Frank Hunter, 1979.
10. Frank Hunter, 1979.
11. From a 1914 postcard view taken by James T. Taggart.
12. Keith Bryant, 1964, courtesy of the Oskaloosa *Herald.*
13. From woodcut in Des Moines *Iowa Homestead,* January 5, 1883.
14. From woodcut in Des Moines *Iowa Homestead,* January 5, 1883.
15. From woodcut in Des Moines *Iowa Homestead,* January 5, 1883.
16. Frank Hunter, 1979.
17. Frank Hunter, 1979.
18. From engraving in *Portrait and Biographical Record of Johnson, Poweshiek and Iowa Counties, Iowa* (Chicago, 1893), facing p. 465.
19. Frank Hunter, 1979.
20. Frank Hunter, 1979.
21. Frank Hunter, 1979.
22. Lowell Soike, 1979.
23. Frank Hunter, 1979.
24. Reprinted from *Seventh Annual Report* of the Wisconsin Agricultural Experiment Station, Madison, 1890.
25. Photo of King courtesy State Historical Society of Wisconsin.
26. Reprinted from *Seventh Annual Report* of the Wisconsin Agricultural Experiment Station, Madison, 1890.
27. Reprinted from Wilber J. Fraser, *The Round Barn* University of Illinois Agricultural Experiment Station, Circular 230 (Urbana, 1918), p. 4.
28. Frank Hunter, 1979.
29. From C. O. Alexander, "A Round Clay-Tile Barn," *American Carpenter and Builder* 15 (June 1913), 64.
30. From *American Carpenter and Builder* 15 (June 1913), 64.
31. From *American Carpenter and Builder* 15 (June 1913), 64.
32. Frank Hunter, 1979.
33. Frank Hunter, 1979.
34. Frank Hunter, 1979.
35. Dick Koerselman, LeMars, 1981.
36. Frank Hunter, 1979.
37. Frank Hunter, 1979.
38. Frank Hunter, 1979.
39. Frank Hunter, 1979.
40. From J. E. Wing, "An Iowa Round Barn," *Breeder's Gazette* 48 (Aug. 16, 1905), 273.
41. Lowell Soike, 1982.
42. From family photo collection of Haven W. Frantz.
43. From Cramlet family photo collection.
44. From Cramlet family photo collection.
45. From Cramlet family photo collection.
46. 1979 view by Frank Hunter.
47. Construction photo from Holtkamp family collection.
48. 1979 view by Frank Hunter.
49. From Matt L. King, "An Umbrella for the Cattle," *American Carpenter and Builder* 23 (June 1917), 54.
50. From *American Carpenter and Builder* 23 (June 1917), 54.
51. From *American Carpenter and Builder* 23 (June 1917), 55.
52. From *American Carpenter and Builder* 17 (April 1914), 68.
53. Benton Steele portrait from family views collected by Linda J. Harsin, Sedgwick, Kansas.
54. Exterior elevation from Waterloo *Kimball's Dairy Farmer* (June 15, 1912), 380.
55. Frank Hunter, 1979.
56. From *Wallaces' Farmer* 28 (Jan. 16, 1903), 74.
57. Frank Hunter, 1979.
58. Photo taken in 1975 Iowa State University Architectural Windshield Survey conducted for the Iowa State Historical Department, Office of Historic Preservation.
59. Frank Hunter, 1979.
60. Catalog plans from Gordon-Van Tine Company *Farm Buildings* (Davenport, 1917), p. 46.
61. Catalog plans from Gordon-Van Tine Company *Farm Buildings* (Davenport, 1917), p. 46.
62. Lowell Soike, 1982.
63. Frank Hunter, 1979.
64. Frank Hunter, 1979.
65. Reprinted from Des Moines *Dairy Farmer* (Aug 1927), 13.
66. Frank Hunter.
67. Karen Gilbertson, Central Iowa Regional Association of Local Governments Architectural Survey, 1978.
68. Bob Dean (KVFD Radio, Fort Dodge), about 1966.
69. Frank Hunter, 1979.
70. From a color slide by Lowell Soike, 1979.
71. Lowell Soike, 1979.
72-73. Rex Flint Kote roofing advertisement from *Wallaces' Farmer* 30 (Mar. 17, 1905), 372; Mica-Noid Ready roofing advertisement from *Wallaces' Farmer* 31 (April 6, 1906), 490.
74. From *Scott County Atlas,* 1919.
75. Frank Hunter, 1979.
76. Jan Reiste Pedley, 1982, courtesy of *Ocheyedan Press — Melvin News.*
77. Dick Koerselman, LeMars, 1981.
78. Frank Hunter, 1979.

Publication has been funded with the assistance of a matching grant-in-aid from the Department of the Interior, National Park Service, under the provisions of the National Historical Preservation Act of 1966 and subsequent amendments. The opinions expressed herein are not necessarily those of the Department of the Interior, National Park Service.

Note to second edition 1990: The barns shown existed in 1983.

Library of Congress Card Catalog Number: 90-62736
ISBN 0-941016-80-3

Production: Lowell Soike and Christie Dailey of the Iowa State Historical Department.
Design and paste-up: Newton C. Burch of the Iowa Department of General Services, Printing Division.
Line drawings: Dennett-Muessig and Associates, Iowa City.

Cover: View of the old Meyer round barn built in 1912. The 56-foot diameter barn is located just south of Waukon in the northeast quarter of section 12, Ludlow Township, Allamakee County. Photo by Lowell J. Soike, 1979.

Back cover: True-Round Barn
Allamakee County Post Township, Section 2
Photo by Joan Liffring-Zug

WITHOUT RIGHT ANGLES

THE ROUND BARNS OF IOWA

Lowell J. Soike

Penfield
Press